Beyond Low-Fat Baking

Cancer Fighting Foods for the Millennium

BEYOND LOW-FAT BAKING
CANCER FIGHTING FOODS FOR THE
MILLENNIUM

100 reduced-fat recipes for scrumptious
and simple-to-make breads, muffins, pizzas,
cakes, cookies, and pies. All include
a nutritional boost.

SHIRLEEN SANDO

PRESIDENT AND FOUNDER
LIVING HEALTHY FOODS

SKYWARD PUBLISHING, INC.

, DALLAS, TEXAS
www.skywardpublishing.com
skyward@sheltonbbs.com

BEYOND LOW-FAT BAKING
CANCER FIGHTING FOODS FOR THE MILLENNIUM

Please consult your doctor with any personal questions about your dietary choices and this book. Shirleen Sando of Living Healthy Foods and Skyward Publishing, Inc. disclaim all liability in connection with the use of this book.

Library of Congress Cataloging-in-Publication Data
Sando, Shirleen, 1948-
     Beyond low-fat baking: cancer fighting foods for the millennium: 100 low-fat recipes for scrumptious and simple-to-make breads, muffins, pizzas, cakes, cookies, pies, and all include a nutritional boost / Shirleen Sando.
          p.   cm.
     ISBN 1-881554-03-1
     1. Low-fat diet Recipes.   2. Baking.   3. Cookery (Tofu)
4. Cancer--Prevention.   5. Cancer--Diet therapy.   I. Title.
RM237.7.S27   2000
641.5 638--dc21   99-30660
                                                                        CIP

Publisher: Skyward Publishing, Inc.
17440 North Dallas Parkway, Suite 100
Dallas, TX 75287
Marketing: 813 Michael Street, Kennett, MO 63857
Phone/fax (573) 717--1040

Dedicated with love to my son Shawn
who was unfortunate enough to have cancer
but fortunate enough to survive and to
my daughter Shelly who I hope will
never face this dreadful disease.
This book should enable them and others to enjoy
cherished foods while protecting their health.

Contents

Acknowledgments

The creation of this book took the dedication and support of many people. My deepest thanks and appreciation go to my husband Larry and my children Shawn and Shelly who allowed me the time and opportunity to make this book possible. I offer a big thank you to my sister Charlotte and my daughter Shelly who tested and sampled many of the recipes in this book. Thank you! Thank you! Thank you!

To my many friends who sampled dozens of breads, cookies, cakes, and pies, I offer my thanks. A special thanks goes to John and Carol Fisher who sampled and evaluated hundreds of recipes and assured me of success and pointed out failures. I can't thank you enough. To my special friends Myra and Eddie Callahan, I offer thanks for all the many cookies and cakes you sampled and for offering advice. I especially thank all of you for the many times you supported my efforts.

I offer a special thank you to Jim Harris who helped me keep the dream alive for this book. From concept to publication, Jim never failed to believe in this project or in me. Without motivation and support from friends, no book would make it to print. Thank you.

I own a great big Thank You to Carol Fisher for her invaluable help in proofing the manuscript and to Sharon Hale for her help in typesetting, editing, and layout of copy.

INTRODUCTION

The use of soy-based food products as a dietary supplement is becoming more common. Both increased agricultural production as well as the health benefits offered by tofu, soy flour, soy milk, and other soyfood sources, have contributed to this escalation.

Soy's most widely known nutritional benefit is the high protein content. This vegetable protein results in a low saturated fat and cholesterol-free dietary protein alternative. Medical research has established conclusively the impact of such a diet on reducing both heart disease and stroke. More recent research has indicated a possible reduction in certain types of cancers, as well.

Soy is also a good source of dietary calcium and natural estrogen-type substance. This could result in a decreased incidence of osteoporosis and subsequent bone fractures with long-term use. Soy, in its many forms, can also be enriched with several vitamins and minerals linked to good health and longevity, such as vitamin D, thiamine, riboflavin, zinc, and iron.

Incorporating soy into our diet is now easier and tastier through publications like Beyond Low-Fat Baking, a book which enables us to reap the benefits of a healthier lifestyle.

Stephen A. Smith, M.D.

Message from the Author

As president and founder of the Living Healthy Food Center, a family-run test kitchen for creating healthier, low-fat and reduced-fat foods that the average family can enjoy, my primary objective was to design dishes that retain all the wonderful flavors we have always relished and cherished. A natural progression from health to disease prevention followed this guideline when my fight became personal. Out of the blue, my twenty-eight year old son was diagnosed with a rare form of cancer of the small intestine. And my father, as a result of eating a high-fat diet for all of his eighty-plus years, had severe liver damage, which forced him to give up his favorite foods before he died.

Thankfully, my son's story has a happy ending. After a grueling fourteen-hour surgery, followed by radiation, chemotherapy, and dietary changes, he has become a cancer survivor. Like many of you, I'm sure, I never thought I would be using those words in connection with someone I love. Cancer is for other people, not for me or my family. Cancer is for middle-aged or older people, not a twenty-eight-year-old. My son was too young!

For those who believe cancer and heart disease are merely a matter of age or bad luck, you need to change your thinking. Research clearly points to diet as part of the armor that you can use to defend yourself and your loved ones in fighting these and other life-threatening ailments. While no one can say for certain that dietary changes will prevent cancer or other deadly diseases, research promises plenty of hope for diet making an impact.

The past few years have witnessed a veritable explosion of interest in cancer-fighting foods. The American Institute for Cancer Research estimates that there are 1.4 million new cases of cancer every year, and every year more than a half million Americans lose their lives to the disease. Furthermore, the American Heart Association reminds us that coronary heart disease is still the leading cause of death in the United States, killing more than 600,000 people yearly.

The *1998 Surgeon General's Report on Nutrition and Health* flatly states that two-thirds of all deaths--including coronary heart disease, stroke, atherosclerosis, diabetes, and some forms of cancer--are related to dietary choices. Many health authorities now believe that approximately 35 percent of all cancer deaths in America may be diet related.

These findings are not entirely new. Scientific studies, dating back to the early eighties, linked diet to possible cancer prevention. A landmark 1982 report from the National Academy of Sciences was the first to identify the link between diet and cancer. The latest Diet and Cancer Project report clearly establishes, "...the foods we choose play an overwhelming role in fighting cancer." A strong statement, indeed.

In *Diet and Cancer Prevention, New Report: New Recommendations Give Hope for the Future,* the American Institute for Cancer Research points out, "Cancer can be prevented. Not every case of cancer, but large enough numbers to have a dramatic impact on today's high cancer incidence and mortality rates." The report explains, "...if people were just to eat the recommended five or more servings of fruits and vegetables each day, overall cancer incidence rates could decline by as much as 20 percent. For some cancers, the effects of dietary change are even more dramatic."

Dr. T. Colin Campbell of Cornell University, the joint chairman of the Diet and Cancer Project, states, "Scientific evidence from more than twenty years of research indicates that a low-fat, plant-based diet can protect against cancer and other chronic disease."

Many health authorities have long asserted that the nutritious unprocessed foods we have been blessed with on this earth contain natural healing properties, and scientific studies now seem to confirm many of these beliefs. Although no fool-proof cures for cancer and heart disease have been found, there is positive hope for reducing their threat. Dr. Dean Ornish's groundbreaking work established important links between dietary choice and heart disease with his research pointing to fat reduction, moderate exercise, and meditation as effective ways to reverse heart disease.

And common ground seems to exist in the field of cancer prevention. Evidence increasingly points to these simple and practical techniques as a positive means of reducing cancer risks. This is, of course, very good news and gives everyone a chance to be proactive in maintaining personal health.

Since soyfoods are some of the most nutritious foods known to humankind, I now cook more soy-based dishes and continue to invent new and unusual ways to incorporate them into our diet. The nourishing qualities of soyfoods have been known for centuries. Americans realize this fact, and we seldom settle for second best, yet in our food choices, we often do just that. Sadly, we raise most of the world's soybeans and ship many to Japan, a country where longevity is common.

Americans are having a reality check. It is reported that 26,000,000 U.S. consumers are now using soy products. Soy consumption is becoming mainstream. Soyfoods are rich in high quality protein, low in fat, and are considered to have a low glycemic index. Soy protein is superior to other plant proteins. Soybeans contain many of the essential fatty acids being studied for improved health. Some health specialists suggest that people with elevated risk of developing diabetes may benefit from soy's low glycemic index. Always check with your doctor or health care practitioner before making any dietary changes.

NOTE: For recipes in *Beyond Low-Fat Baking*, I use low-fat silken tofu, 1% fat per serving.

TOFU FOR GOOD HEALTH

Tofu is perhaps the perfect fat replacement for baking. It is high in protein, low in fat, and very easy to digest. While providing the desired moistness in breads and other baked goods, tofu imparts richness, texture, and taste.

Although tofu is bland and has little flavor of its own, it picks up the flavor of other foods. When added to chocolate, for example, tofu picks up the flavor of chocolate. In cheesecake, tofu absorbs the flavor of the cream cheese.

The increased nutrition in tofu laced baked goods is a welcome plus for anyone desiring more vitamins, protein, and minerals in the diet. Who among us doesn't? Yet, many reduced fat recipes actually decrease protein and other nutrients. In an effort to cut the fat in baked goods, many low-fat recipes exclude egg yolks, yet egg yolks, though cholesterol rich, contain valuable protein and other essential nutrients.

Substituting egg whites in place of whole eggs, many lower fat cookbooks offer lower fat or fat-free treats, yet this fat reduction method does nothing to increase nutrition. By comparison, *Beyond Low-Fat Baking* shows you how to expand the healthy baking concept. To cook healthier baked goods, eliminate part of the fat and replace it with easy-to-use vitamin-and-mineral-rich tofu. And it's so easy. Simply remove tofu from its container. Drain and mash it or blend in a blender and use in your favorite recipes. As a bonus, any leftover portions can be refrigerated and added later to soups and casseroles or used to make delicious and satisfying tofu milk shakes. Tofu-enriched baked goods contain vitamins A, B, C, D, E, high-quality protein, and minerals such as iron and calcium. The highest levels of calcium are found in tofu when the curdling agent used to make the tofu is a calcium salt.

As a plus, low-fat tofu is extremely low in saturated fat and contains no cholesterol. While 50 percent of the calories in tofu come from fat, a 4-ounce serving has only 6 grams of fat. Tofu can be purchased in reduced-fat forms that contain just 1 percent fat per serving. (As a general rule, the softer the tofu, the lower the fat content.) **Recipes in *Beyond Low-Fat Baking* use 1 percent silken fat tofu.**

Since tofu is low in sodium, it is a perfect food for those on a sodium-restricted diet. (To help you better understand the value of eating a soy-food-based diet, see the special section entitled "More About Soy," which explains the latest research concerning the health benefits of soy.)

Adding soy flour is another way of increasing nutrition in baked items without changing taste. Soy flour is an excellent source of vitamins and minerals, including iron, calcium, and B vitamins. Adding soy flour, tofu, or soymilk to baked goods is not really a new concept. Professional bakers have long known that these ingredients actually improve the quality of bread dough, making for a more tender texture and excellent taste. *Beyond Low-Fat Baking* shares these bakers' secrets with you, allowing you to serve your family and friends rich-tasting, high-quality baked goods that are virtually indistinguishable from the fat-laden, cholesterol-rich goodies that most of us have been eating for years.

KEEP THE TASTE

With the recipes in *Beyond Low-Fat Baking*, none of the tasty stuff is sacrificed, and most of the bad is gone. These recipes offer an array of fresh-baked favorites, such as Cinnamon Rolls, Decadent Chocolate Cake, Ginger Muffins, Italian Crescent Rolls, and Amaretto Cheesecake. As a special bonus in this book, we at Living Healthy Foods are pleased to include an award-winning recipe from the Missouri Soybean Association.

The step-by-step recipes in *Beyond Low-Fat Baking* will enable you to serve baked goods and sweets that actually contribute to good health. We don't recommend that you increase your consumption of cake and cookies. We merely suggest that by adding soy-based foods to your baked goods you can preserve taste while offering vital nutrients the body needs.

We think your entire family will enjoy these velvety-tasting baked goods. Unless you tell them, they won't know they are eating something that is good for them. These treats are satisfying, delicious, and fun to make.

I wish you the best of luck and hope that cooking becomes the same adventure for you as it has for me. Bon appetit!

THE STANDARD AMERICAN DIET

SAD is an accurate and unfortunate acronym for the Standard American Diet. On average, Americans consume too many calories, too much fat, too much cholesterol, and too much sodium. To make matters worse, our protein consumption comes mainly from animal origin, and studies now indicate that excessive amounts of animal protein may place us at health risk.

A study of the Food Guide Pyramid, put out by the United States Department of Agriculture, clearly suggests that the mainstay of our diet should be complex carbohydrates from such plant foods as fruits, vegetables, and grains. A diet too low in plant-based foods can spur the development of life-threatening deficiencies, perhaps even causing cancer and heart disease. (When your mother insisted that you eat your fruits and vegetables, she instinctively knew what was good for you.)

If that isn't a good enough reason to enjoy them, foods high in complex carbohydrates are often less fattening than many other foods simply because they inherently contain less fat. Breads, quick breads, and muffins of all sorts fall into this category because they are made of the complex carbohydrates we need if we are to reach and maintain optimum health.

SOYBEAN PROTEIN: A KEY TO GOOD HEALTH

Protein is, of course, important in our diet. Protein is part of the key to good health. Most of our body is made of protein, from the brain on down. Our blood, heart, lungs, tendons, ligaments, nerves, muscles, hair, skin, and nails are all made of protein tissues. Even teeth require protein. About one-third of the body's protein is in our muscles, about one-fifth is in the bones and cartilage, about one-tenth is in the skin, and the rest is in other tissues and bodily fluids.

Maintaining a healthy balance of protein means consuming protein. Unfortunately, in the United States, "protein" is usually synonymous with meat and dairy. According to scientific research, a healthier source of protein is soybean based. With research pointing to saturated fat as a health hazard–and meat is, of course, high in saturated fat–many smart, health-conscious people are turning to soy protein as a healthy alternative to meat-and dairy-based foods.

THE SOY WAY TO PERFECT HEALTH

As an alternative to animal protein, it is easy to get complete protein from mature legumes (beans and peas), including dried peas and soybeans, English walnuts, and peanuts. Be aware that walnuts and peanuts are higher in saturated fat.

As a protein source, soy protein outclasses all others. In fact, soy-based protein is so completely balanced—more than the protein in other beans and peas—that researchers believe adults could indefinitely satisfy their protein needs mainly with soy.

PHYTOCHEMICALS

The addition of soy to the diet is believed to actually improve health in a number of ways. Scientists have long known that food contains vitamins, minerals, and other essential nutrients and that those nutrients promote health. In recent years, new classes of compounds have been found in food.

These compounds are different from other nutrients. Researchers are just now unlocking the keys as to how these compounds affect health. Called phytochemicals, these compounds are found only in plant-based, not animal-based, food sources.

ISOFLAVONES

Scientists now tell us that although all plant foods have phytochemicals, only soy contains a high amount of a phytochemical called isoflavone. This substance—sometimes referred to as *phytoestrogen,* or plant estrogen—has been isolated and studied for possible ways to prevent disease. Therefore, if you avoid isoflavone-rich soy products, you're avoiding food sources that could possibly prevent some diseases, including heart disease.

Just how is such prevention possible? Studies indicate that isoflavones aid in slowing or preventing blood clots—and a tendency to form blood clots may increase the risk of heart attack and heart disease. (*Genistein* is the isoflavone compound that scientists believe has the ability to reduce the development of harmful cells that can build up and block arteries.) Soy protein has recently been shown to reduce blood-cholesterol levels and to reduce the risk of premature heart disease in some cases.

MAKE HEALTHY FAT CHOICES

Fats in their pure chemical state are colorless, odorless, and tasteless. Most of the natural fats Americans consume contain traces of other substances which provide flavor. Over the last decade, we have heard much talk about saturated and unsaturated fats, and more Americans have become fat educated. Fats are a concern because the amount of fat used by most Americans has increased steadily during most of the twentieth century. By the mid-sixties, the average American was eating close to 50% of calories from fat.

Even with new information available on the dangers of excessive fat in our diets, many are still over eating saturated fat in one form or another. Since fast-food restaurants continue to turn a hefty profit, and their menus feature many items that are high in saturated fat, one could logically assume that despite all the education and warnings, Americans still consume way too much unhealthy fat.

As a guide, the American Heart Association recommends that our total fat intake be less than 30 percent of daily calories. Many health authorities recommend an even lower percentage of fat in the diet, recommending fat intake stay around the twenty percent range.

A three ounce serving of oven roasted beef has 35 grams of fat per serving. Three slices of pizza, sold in popular pizza parlors, contain approximately 30 grams or more of fat. A hamburger can contain 23 grams or more depending on size. Many fast food items contain from 16 to 30 or more grams of fat per item. Since butter has14 grams of fat per tablespoon, adding 1-2 tablespoons of butter on a roll increases the fat an additional 14 to 28 grams. The same principle applies to salad dressing. We are not just talking about obesity here. We are talking about high cholesterol, cancer, and heart attack.

REPLENISH YOUR EFAs DAILY

While saturated fat is unhealthy, some fat is essential to health and needs to be replenished daily. When the body is deficient in essential fatty acids (nutritionists tell us), we risk damage to skin, become infertile, heal poorly, and become mentally sluggish.

The Food and Agricultural Organization and the World Health Organization suggest that adults consume a minimum of 3 percent of total calories as essential fatty acids (EFAs). That means if you eat a 2,000-calorie-per-day diet, at least 60 of your daily calories, or 6.7 grams, should come from EFAs. The secret is obtaining the right kind of fat in the right portions. Always remember that a little fat goes a long way.

Essential fatty acids are necessary for cells to absorb vitamins A and E, which cannot be effectively absorbed without fat. Avoid making the mistake of taking these nutrients in supplement form without acquiring sufficient EFAs. Based on the degree of saturation a fat contains, fatty acids fall into three broad categories. The degree of saturation depends on the composition of links in the chain of carbon from which they are made. Fully saturated fatty acids are found in foods primarily of animal origin and products such as palm oil, palm kernel oil, coconut oil, and cocoa butter. These products are commonly used to make commercially processed foods such as cookies and cakes. Excessive saturated fat has been linked to elevated blood cholesterol levels.

Healthier groups of fatty acids are omega-3 and omega-6. Current research indicates Americans may need more of these fatty acids in the diet. In humans, omega-3 fatty acids are changed into substances that are thought to reduce blood pressure, triglycerides, and cholesterol levels. Omega-3 fatty acids are found in beans, leafy green vegetables, soyfoods, flaxseed, linseed, evening primrose, borage, black current seed oils, and fish oils, such as those found in cod, mackerel, salmon, sardine, and trout. Nuts and seeds are excellent sources of omega-6.

SATURATED FAT AND HEALTH RISK

Excess fat isn't just a physique problem. Evidence suggests that excessive saturated fat in the diet makes the liver produce LDL (bad) cholesterol in quantities greater than the body can remove. This results in damage to the arterial walls, causing atheroclerosis--a disease that impairs the cardiovascular system and increases the risk of heart disease.

While doctors once recommended polyunsaturated fat as the fat of choice, they now recommend using a variety of oils and increasing those that contain higher levels of monounsaturated (healthier) fat. Monounsaturated fats are found in olive, canola, and soy oils. When incorporated into baking, **olive oil** and **soy oil** are excellent choices for making breads. **Canola oil** and **soy oil** are better choices for cakes, cookies, and pies since these oils have a more neutral taste.

Besides decreasing arterial health risks, these oils offer other health benefits. Olive oil and soy oil contain antioxidants (like vitamin E) that actually protect cells from damage. Studies suggest that antioxidant-rich oils aid in controlling free radicals, which have been associated with many diseases as well as with aging.

FAT RUNDOWN

	Saturated	Monounsaturated	Polyunsaturated
Coconut Oil	92%	8%	0%
Palm Kernel Oil	81%	11%	2%
Butter	59%	37%	4%
Palm Oil	50%	32%	18%
Lard	38%	52%	10%
Cottonseed Oil	25%	16%	59%
Crisco	25%	49%	26%
Peanut Oil	23%	46%	31%
Soybean Oil	16%	21%	63%
Sesame Oil	14%	40%	42%
Olive Oil	12%	81%	7%
Corn Oil	11%	31%	58%
Sunflower Oil	10%	20%	66%
Safflower Oil	10%	12%	78%
Canola	6%	62%	32%

This chart clearly shows that coconut oil is highest in unhealthy saturated fat.

USING TOFU

Psychologists tell us we eat baked goods, especially desserts, such as cakes, cinnamon rolls, and pies, because we find them psychologically fulfilling. Americans love comfort food. When feeling depressed or deprived, we turn to chocolate brownies, oatmeal cookies, or other tasty treats because these foods make us feel better. While food addictions can occur from such misuse of food, with some eating an entire bag of double fudgey cookies, other people eat only one or two and get the same psychological lift. If you find yourself with a sweet tooth from time to time, make those sweets more healthful and satisfying by enriching them with soyfoods. Your taste buds will never know the difference between the food you are now eating and those made with nutritious soy.

TOFU AS A CALCIUM SOURCE

Tofu can be an excellent source of calcium. A one half cup serving contains from 80 to 430 mg. calcium. Contents vary depending on the way tofu is processed. Tofu made with calcium sulfate contains the highest level of calcium. To meet personal calcium needs, I, at times, use tofu that is higher in calcium even though it may contain a bit more fat. To increase calcium in the diet, include this easy soy protein shake. In a blender, mix 1 cup nonfat milk, 1/4 cup tofu, and 2-3 large strawberries. Blend. If desired, sweeten with honey or sugar to taste. Any fruit can replace the strawberries. Bananas or peaches are great.

BUYING AND STORING TOFU

Tofu, which is generally found in the produce section of the grocery store, is commonly sold in water-filled tubs, vacuum packs, or aseptic brick packages. Unless aseptically packaged, tofu should be kept refrigerated. As with any perishable food, check the expiration date on the package.

Once opened, tofu should be covered and stored in the refrigerator. It's important to use tofu within a few days after the package is opened. If you buy water-packed tofu, store leftover portions in the refrigerator covered with water. Change water daily.

For short-term storage, I drain unused portions of aseptically packaged tofu, mash it, and store in an airtight container in the refrigerator. This storage method, which is good for a day or two, allows for ready use in biscuits, cakes, pancakes, waffles, and breads.

TOFU AS A FAT SUBSTITUTE

When tofu is used with fat ingredients, like butter, shortening, or oil, always cream the tofu and fat together. (For calculations of fat content in these recipes, I used 1 percent fat tofu unless otherwise specified in a recipe.) If sugar is called for in the recipe, I often combine it with the fat and tofu mixture. When used in smooth desserts, like cheesecake, tofu should be creamed thoroughly in a food processor or blender. (Even a mini-processor will nicely blend tofu, turning it into a creamy texture.) When used in cakes, cookies, and pies, any tiny granules of tofu will blend with other ingredients as the dessert bakes. For many recipes, tofu is simply removed from the package, drained and mashed, and added to the recipe.

TYPES OF TOFU

Generally, three main types of tofu are available in American grocery stores. The softer kinds are best for blending, mashing, and crumbling. Be aware that tofu does not work well with some dishes such as soufflés.

♦ Firm tofu is dense and solid and holds up well in stir-fry dishes, soups, or on the grill—anywhere that you want the tofu to maintain its shape. Firm tofu is also higher in protein, fat, and calcium than other forms of tofu.

♦ Soft tofu is a good choice for recipes that call for blended tofu or for use in soups.

♦ Silken tofu, made by a slightly different process, has a creamy, custard-like texture. Silken tofu works well in pureed or blended dishes and baking. In Japan, silken tofu is enjoyed, as is, with a touch of soy sauce and topped with chopped scallions. **NOTE: I use low-fat silken tofu, 1% fat per serving in all recipes.**

See the appendix for more soy information.

The following chart is intended for informational use only.

NUTRIENTS IN FOUR OUNCES OF TOFU

	Firm Tofu	Soft Tofu	Silken Tofu
Calories	120	86	72
Protein (grams)	13	9	9.6
Carbohydrates (grams)	3	2	3.2
Fat (grams)	6	5	2.4
Saturated fat (grams)	1	1	0
Cholesterol	0	0	0
Sodium (milligrams)	9	8	76
Fiber (grams)	1	0	0
Calcium (milligrams)	120	130	40
Iron (milligrams)	8	7	1
% calories from protein	43	39	53
% calories from carbohydrates	10	9	17
%of calories from fat	45	52	30

Sources: Composition of Foods: Legumes and Legume Products. United States Department of Agriculture, Human Nutrition Information Service, Agriculture Handbook 8-16, revised December 1986, and from product analysis.

NOTE: *1 percent fat per serving tofu is used in recipes in this book.*

SOY MILK AS A DAIRY SUBSTITUTE

The Soyfoods Association of America, funded by the United Soybean Board, provides the following information concerning soy milk. Soy milk is the rich milk of whole soybeans. It provides all the nutrition of soybeans--protein, minerals, vitamins, iron, omega-3, and essential fatty acids. With its unique nutty flavor, soy milk can be used in a variety of ways. In China and Japan, fresh soy milk is made daily using a simple, centuries old process of grinding soaked and cooked soybeans and pressing the dissolved soy milk out of the beans. In these countries, soy milk is sold by street vendors or in cafes. These Eastern cultures serve it hot or cold and often serve it as a sweetened beverage. For a spicy soup, they flavor soy milk with soy sauce, onions, and vegetables. You can also heat vanilla flavored soy milk with cinnamon, ginger, or other spices and drink it hot. Plain soy milk can be used in place of dairy milk in most recipes.

SOY FLOUR: A NEW AMERICAN STAPLE

Soy flour should be found in every kitchen in America. This versatile flour can be easily added to almost any dessert or bread that is cooked or baked. Soy flour, which is made from roasted soybeans that have been ground into a fine powder, is rich in high-quality protein and other nutrients. Contrary to what many believe—if used in the right proportions—soy flour does *not* change the taste. If too much is used, a slight beany taste does occur. The secret is keeping the right proportion of soy flour to all-purpose or whole wheat flour. Two tablespoons of soy flour can generally be substituted for two tablespoons of all-purpose without changing taste.

Two kinds of soy flour are readily available--full-fat and defatted. Both kinds of soy flour will give a protein boost to recipes; however, the protein in defatted soy flour is even more concentrated than in full-fat soy flour.

Tip: Like all whole-grain flours, both defatted and full-fat soy flour should be stored in the refrigerator or freezer.

SOY FLOUR NUTRITIONAL VALUE PER 3.5 OUNCES (by weight)

	Full-fat, roasted	Defatted
Calories	441	329
Protein	34.8	47
Fat	21	1.2
Carbohydrates	33.7	38.4
Fiber	2.2	4.3
Calcium	188	241
Iron	5.8	9.2
Zinc	3.5	2.4
Thiamin (B1)	41	7
Riboflavin	.94	.25
Niacin	3.29	2.61

"Composition of Foods: Legume and Legume Products," Agriculture Handbook, Number 8–16, revised December 1986, United States Department of Agriculture, Human Nutrition Information Service.

EAT MORE GRAINS

The American Medical Association and the American Institute of Cancer Research recommend eating a wide variety of foods to insure that both macronutrients and micronutrients are adequately supplied in the diet. A good way to get these nutrients is from grains. While soy flour or tofu is used in every recipe in *Beyond Low-Fat Baking,* I have also included many recipes that use other grains. My test kitchen is well stocked with grains listed in this book, and I have experimented with all of them. As long as the proportions are in balance with higher gluten flours, like wheat, the final products are delicious and healthier than those made only with all-purpose flour, the kind most American cooks rely on today.

ALL- PURPOSE FLOUR

All-purpose flour, which is made from wheat, is most often used in baking because it contains the most gluten, a protein that forms bread's structure. Don't confuse wheat gluten with gluten flour. The gluten available at health-food stores and some supermarkets is called *vital gluten,* a product that improves the texture and rise of whole-grain breads.

All-purpose flour can be purchased in both unbleached and bleached versions. Bleached flour undergoes an aging process that whitens it, and some nutritionists suggest bleaching agents may be harmful. Unbleached flour is recommended in *Beyond Low-Fat Baking.* In bread machine recipes, I often use bread machine flour, a gluten–packed flour that insures a good rise in these special breads.

FIBER, FIBER, FIBER

To restore the fiber and other important nutrients that are lost in the milling process, it's best to use at least some whole-wheat, soy, or other whole-grain flour in baking. With all the emphasis over the past few years on lower fat eating, many of us seem to have forgotten the importance of a fiber-rich diet. Fiber pushes food through the body. Some nutritionists suggest it cleans the intestine by scouring away toxins in the colon.

A fiber-rich diet helps maintain your waistline because fiber absorbs water, thereby, making you feel full. Most of the fiber is then passed from the body. As important, recent research indicates that fiber is yet another weapon in the anti-cancer arsenal. Although the American Cancer Institute recommends eating 25 to 30 grams of fiber per day, statistics suggest that most of us get half or even less of that amount.

WHOLE-GRAINS PACK IN NUTRITION

If you have been following cooking trends lately, you may have noticed that some of today's best-known chefs are adding soy flour, blue-corn flour, and other specialty grains to favorite recipes. Americans love the taste of this new cuisine, and millions are learning to cook with these foods at home.

Beyond taste, whole-grains provide a great nutritional punch. Whole-grains are both fiber rich and nutrient rich. Nutrients—especially in the form of complex carbohydrates—provide energy that keeps us going throughout the day. Whole-grains also provide an abundance of vitamins, minerals, and antioxidants (such as vitamin E), vitamin B-6, folate, zinc, copper, magnesium, selenium, chromium, and a wide range of other nutrients that some scientists believe aid in fighting disease.

TYPES OF GRAINS

Each whole-grain offers a unique taste and/or benefit.

Amaranth Flour: Amaranth, a broad-leafed plant, produces seeds that can be ground, like grains, into flour. Amaranth is higher than most grains in protein. It is rich in amino acids, lysine, and methionine, all of which are deficient in beans. Amaranth is, therefore, an important flour to use more often in baked goods.

Blue-Corn Flour: This popular southwestern flour (already familiar to fans of blue-corn tortilla chips) is rapidly becoming more common on American tables, especially when cooks are looking for unique ways to make wholesome pancakes and waffles. Low-fat potassium-rich blue-corn flour contains the rich goodness of corn while providing a heartier, rugged taste.

Flaxseed Meal: Flaxseed, prized by the ancient Egyptians, is being studied as a potent health food. High in omega-3, flaxseed naturally reduces cholesterol and is also being studied for its natural estrogenic activity. Ground flaxseed meal can partially replace cooking oil in baked goods.

Generally, you can use a three-to-one ratio when substituting flaxseed in baked goods. For example, 1 1/2 cups of ground flaxseed easily cuts the need for each half cup of butter, margarine, or cooking oil in some recipes. To boost nutrition in baked goods, I often add smaller amounts of flaxseed meal to cakes, cookies, and breads, replacing 1 to 2 tablespoons of refined flour with 1 to 2 tablespoon of flaxseed meal. No one will notice the smaller addition of this healthy ingredient unless you tell them.

Oats: Besides whole-wheat flour (which contains the entire wheat kernel) and soya powder or soy flour (which is concentrated in vitamins and minerals), using whole-grain oats can be another valuable addition to breads. Those great muscle-building oats contain seven B vitamins and vitamin E, as well as supplying nine minerals: iron, calcium, magnesium, sodium, potassium, phosphorus, copper, manganese, and zinc.

Since oat flour is low in gluten, you need to use this grain with gluten-rich wheat flour when making a high-rise, moist loaf.

When baking cookies and quick bread, use only old-fashioned and quick-cooking oats; save the instant oatmeal for breakfast cereals. To make whole-grain oat flour, blend 1/2 to 1 cup uncooked oats. Process one minute. Store flour in a tightly covered container in a cool, dry place, or freeze for longer storage. To add fiber and other nutrients to baked goods, use 1 to 2 tablespoons of oat flour in place of an equal amount of all-purpose flour. Oat flour works best in desserts that rely on heavy additions of applesauce, tofu, or fruit to help keep them moist because oat flour can make products a bit crumbly.

Soy Flour: Soy flour is made by grinding soybeans. Defatted soy flour is soy flour that has had most of the fat removed. Soy flour contains 40 to 60 percent protein. The protein in soy and wheat complement each other to form a complete vegetable protein. Soy flour is rich in dietary fiber, potassium, calcium, iron, and zinc. It contains vitamin A and many important B vitamins. Soy flour is especially rich in heart-healthy folacin, containing 289 mg per one-cup serving.

Professional bakers have long been aware of soy flour's ability to condition dough, making it rise better. The amount needed is only 1 teaspoon per cup of wheat flour.

Spelt: An ancient grain, spelt, appeared about 9,000 years ago, with many believing it first appeared in southwest Asia. Still cultivated by farmers in Bavaria, spelt is valuable for its high-fiber and high-protein content. An added benefit, spelt is an excellent alternative for those allergic to wheat.

Spelt kernels are nutritious because the kernels contain all the original nutrients. While there are cookbooks devoted to cooking entirely with spelt, our aim is simply to show you how to use spelt as a partial substitute for wheat flour in a few recipes. For an energy boost, replace 1 to 2 tablespoons of wheat flour with spelt in many of your favorite recipes.

Quinoa: Quinoa (pronounced *keen' wa*) stands alone as a complete protein grain, supplying all the essential amino acids in a balanced pattern. Although quinoa adds rich flavor, this flour lacks gluten and needs to be used in conjunction with other flours in breads.

Kamut: This ancient strain of wheat (pronounced *ka moot'*) is gaining popularity. Kamut flour may be partially substituted for wheat flour in most recipes. Because kamut tends to have a lower moisture content than wheat, you may need to add a bit more liquid to bread recipes. For every cup of kamut flour substituted for whole wheat, increase liquid by 1 tablespoon.

SPECIALTY PRODUCT

Tofu Powder: Tofu powder is high in lean protein, containing 10 grams per quarter-cup serving. The same serving size has 1.5 grams of fat, 0 grams saturated fat, 5 mg of sodium, 65 mg of potassium, and 4.5 grams of fiber. Tofu powder, which can be purchased in many health-food stores, is excellent in breads if you enjoy a slightly firm texture. To use tofu powder in regular bread recipes, substitute 1 to 2 tablespoons per cup to replace the same amount of unbleached flour.

NUTRITIONAL COMPARISONS OF THREE POPULAR WHOLE GRAINS

❑ When it comes to potassium, for each one-cup serving, whole-wheat flour (486 mg) is higher than all-purpose white flour (134 mg), while soy flour (2113 mg) is the highest of all.

❑ Since potassium helps to balance sodium in the diet, and many Americans consume too much sodium, potassium is an important nutrient to use when fortifying food. Adding even small amounts of soy flour to a recipe will increase potassium in the diet.

Soy is the only flour containing the essential fatty acid, linoleic acid. Soy is also higher in protein, containing 29 grams per one-cup serving. Whole-wheat flour contains 16 grams, and all-purpose flour contains12 grams.

Per one-cup serving, soy flour contains 8.1 grams of dietary fiber. Whole-wheat flour contains 14.6 grams, and all-purpose flour contains 3.6 grams of dietary fiber per serving.

Soy flour and whole-wheat flour contain appreciable amounts of zinc, with soy flour averaging 3.3 grams per cup, whole-wheat flour 3.5 grams, and all-purpose flour dropping to less than 1 gram.

Of the three flours, soy is the only one that contains vitamin A. Soy flour is also extremely rich in high-quality protein and is an excellent source of iron, calcium, and B vitamins. With a recent health focus on the B vitamin folacin as an important nutrient in lowering coronary risk, it is important to note that soy flour contains 289 mcg of folacin. Whole-wheat flour drops to 31 mcg and all-purpose to 32 mcg of folacin.

STORING WHOLE-GRAINS

To protect flour from absorbing moisture, store all flours in airtight containers. Specialty flours that contain some of the germ of the grain should be refrigerated or placed in the freezer because the oil in the germ will eventually turn flour rancid.

Tip: Before using refrigerated flour, allow it to warm to room temperature. If soy flour is lumpy, measure and then sift.

ADD NUTS TO BAKED GOODS

Adding nuts to bread or other baked goods must be a choice. True, nuts contain a variety of nutrients including protein, yet they are well known for a high fat content. Pecans are traditionally added to bread, but hazelnuts have excellent nutrients that are missing in pecans. Pecans, walnuts, hazelnuts, and almonds vary in fat content.

Pecans per one-cup serving contain 3.1 grams of saturated fat, 24.1 grams of monounsaturated fat, and 9.6 grams of polyunsaturated fat--a total of 37.1 grams of fat.

Walnuts per one-cup serving contain 1.1 grams of saturated fat, 3.6 grams of monounsaturated fat, and 11.3 grams of polyunsaturated fat--a total of 16 grams of fat.

Almonds per one-cup serving contain 2.8 grams of saturated fat, 19.3 grams of monounsaturated fat, and 6.2 grams of polyunsaturated fat--a total of 28.3 gams of fat.

Clearly, walnuts contain less fat than pecans and almonds. Walnuts contain less saturated fat and more polyunsaturated fat. Almonds rank second in saturated fat content, and pecans contain the highest level.

Remember that most health specialists rank saturated fat as the least healthy and monounsaturated as the most healthy, but fat is fat and if weight control is a concern, it is necessary to reduce fat intake.

No-Fuss
Machine
Breads

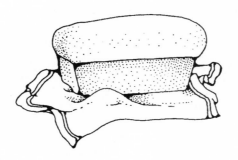

MACHINE BREADS

For no-fuss bread making at home, a bread machine is an essential tool. A bread machine allows you to experience the pleasure of creating nutritious, hearty, delicious aromatic breads while eliminating most of the work.

Tofu and soy flour are easily added to traditional bread machine recipes. Soy flour is simply added with all-purpose flour. Tofu is mashed and added to the machine first. Then follow directions for the bread machine. (Since tofu spoils, it must be refrigerated. Never use a delayed timer when using tofu *or* dairy products of any kind in bread machine recipes.) Just be sure when using recipes from this book to place ingredients in the bread machine in the exact order listed. Mixing of ingredients before processing will spoil finished products. Note: **Use only low-fat silken tofu.**

For extra nutrition and grain variety, add grains such as amaranth, rye, quinoa, and whole-wheat to bread machines. These grains have a variety of both known and unknown nutrients. Continuing research suggests we need whole-grains to keep our bodies strong and healthy. Amaranth easily replaces part of the regular flour in bread recipes with little or no notice in taste. Quinoa slightly alters the taste of breads, but it has its own distinct, delicious flavor. Of course, whole-wheat and rye have long been used in the Western world, making rich, rough-textured, hearty breads.

As a personal preference, I often use the dough setting. I then remove dough, shape it, and allow it to rise a second time before baking in a conventional oven. This method produces lighter and better-textured breads. Sometimes, for convenience, I allow dough to mix, rise, and bake in the bread machine.

It is best to bring all ingredients to room temperature before placing them in a bread machine. Allow whole-grain flour to sit out for a few hours if stored in the refrigerator or freezer. Eggs should stay at room temperature no longer than 30 minutes.

Tofu packaged in an aseptic box should be opened and used directly from the box. If tofu has been refrigerated, simply let it sit out for 10 to 15 minutes in a cool room. Keep in mind that tofu, like dairy products, spoils easily, so avoid leaving out too long.

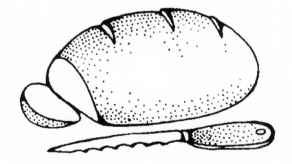

WHOLE-WHEAT BREAD

Hearty and healthy, whole-wheat bread is best accompanied by molasses or honey.

1/4 cup tofu, drained and mashed
1 1/4 cups water
2 tablespoons olive oil
1 3/4 cups bread flour
1 cup whole-wheat flour
1/4 cup vital gluten
2 tablespoons granulated sugar
1 teaspoon salt
2 teaspoons yeast

Select 2-pound loaf size.

Add ingredients to machine in the above order. Bake according to manufacturer's directions. Remove hot bread carefully.

Yield: 12 servings

Do NOT use delayed timer for this recipe.

This is a vegan recipe.

Nutrition Per Serving
Calories: 141
Total fat: 2.7 g
Cholesterol: 0
Carbohydrates: 25 g
Dietary fiber: 1.9 g
Protein: 5.2 g

Health Benefit: Whole wheat bread is fiber-rich and contains many important B vitamins.

CLASSIC WHITE BREAD

This soft-textured bread is wholesome and tender. It is especially delicious when dripping with honey or strawberry jelly.

1 1/4 cups water
2 tablespoons olive oil
2 3/4 cups bread flour
1/4 cup vital gluten
2 tablespoons tofu powder
2 tablespoons granulated sugar
1 teaspoon salt
2 teaspoons yeast

Select 2-pound loaf size.

Add ingredients to bread machine in the above order. Bake according to manufacturer's directions. Remove hot bread carefully.

Yield: 12 servings

You can use the delayed timer for this bread since it uses tofu powder rather than regular tofu.

This is a vegan recipe.

Nutrition Per Serving
Calories: 146
Total fat: 2.6 g
Cholesterol: 0
Carbohydrates: 25 g
Dietary fiber: 1 g
Protein: 5 g

Health Benefit: Although moist and delicious, this bread contains less than 1 gram of fat per serving.

FLUFFY POTATO ROLLS

Fluffy, fluffy, fluffy best describes these scrumptious rolls.

1/2 cup tofu, drained and mashed
1 1/3 cups reserved potato water
2 tablespoons olive oil
1 egg
2 teaspoons salt
3 tablespoons granulated sugar
3/4 cup potatoes (mashed)
4 1/2 cups bread flour
2 teaspoons active dry yeast

Select 2-pound loaf size. Boil and drain potatoes, reserving liquid. Cool potato water to room temperature. Mash potatoes. Add ingredients to bread machine in above order. Select the dough setting.

When dough cycle is complete, turn dough onto a floured surface. Gently work in flour until dough can be easily handled. Shape into balls. Place balls in muffin tins coated with nonstick cooking spray. Cover with a towel and let rise until doubled, approximately 1½ hours.

Preheat oven to 350°F. Bake 15 to 18 minutes. Serve warm. Yield: 24 rolls

Variation: *Substitute 1/2 cup bread flour with 1/2 cup quinoa flour.*
Do NOT use delayed timer for this recipe.

Nutrition Per Serving
Calories: 113
Total fat: 1.8 g
Cholesterol: 8 mg
Carbohydrates: 21 g
Dietary fiber: 0.8 g
Protein: 3.4 g

Health Benefit: Potatoes are a rich source of potassium.

OATMEAL BREAD

(Recipe courtesy of Indiana Soybean Development Council)
A heart-healthy bread that stays moist and delicious.

3/4 cup water
3/4 cup soy milk (plain or vanilla)
1 1/2 tablespoons light butter or margarine
1/3 cup oatmeal
3 cups bread flour
1/3 cup soy flour
1 1/2 teaspoons salt
3 tablespoons granulated sugar
1 1/2 teaspoons dry yeast

Select 2-pound loaf size.

Add ingredients to machine in the above order. Bake according to manufacturer's directions. Remove hot bread carefully.

Yield: 12 servings

Do NOT use delayed timer for this recipe.

Nutrition Per Serving
Calories: 166
Total fat: 1.5 g
Cholesterol: 0
Carbohydrates: 32 g
Dietary fiber: 0.6 g
Protein: 6.5 g

Health Benefit: Oats are well known for their cholesterol lowering ability.

AMARANTH DINNER ROLLS

Tender, moist, and delicious

1/2 cup tofu, drained and mashed
3/4 cup water
4 tablespoons olive oil
2 eggs, beaten
5 tablespoons sugar
1 1/2 teaspoons salt
3 1/2 cups unbleached all-purpose flour
1/2 cup amaranth flour
1/4 cup vital gluten
2 teaspoons active dry yeast

Select 2-pound loaf size.

Add ingredients to machine in above order. Select dough setting. When dough cycle is complete, remove dough. Form into balls. Place on a baking sheet coated with nonstick cooking spray.

Cover and let rise 40-50 minutes or until doubled in bulk.

Preheat oven to 350°F. Bake 20-25 minutes. Serve hot.

Do NOT use delayed timer for this recipe.
Your bread machine must have a dough setting to make this bread.

Yield: 36 servings

Nutrition Per Serving
Calories: 182
Total fat: 4.7 g
Cholesterol: 23 mg.
Carbohydrates: 28 g
Dietary fiber: 1.2 g.
Protein: 6.2 g

Health Benefit: Amaranth flour is a treasure trove of nutrition. It is high in complex carbohydrates. A complete vegetable-grain protein, it is calcium and iron rich.

ONION BREADSTICKS

Spiced with onion, these breadsticks are easily made with a bread machine. Any Italian meal will have a more authentic touch with this delicious accompaniment.

1 cup warm water
1/4 cup tofu, drained and mashed
2 tablespoons olive oil
1 teaspoon salt
1/4 cup vital gluten
2 cups unbleached all-purpose flour
2 tablespoons soy flour
2 teaspoons bread machine yeast

Add ingredients to bread machine in the above order. Select dough setting.

When dough cycle is complete, turn dough onto a floured surface. The dough will be wet and sticky. Gently work in flour until the dough can be easily handled.

Shape dough into breadsticks. Place on backsides (for more room) of cookie sheets coated with nonstick cooking spray. Brush breadsticks with olive oil. If desired, sprinkle tops with additional minced onion flakes or garlic powder. Cover and let rise until doubled, about 1 1/2 hours.

Preheat oven to 450°F. Bake 13 to 15 minutes or until barely golden brown. Carefully remove to wire racks to cool.
Yield: 20 breadsticks

Nutrition Per Serving
Calories: 70
Total fat: 1.6 g
Cholesterol: 0
Carbohydrates: 10 g
Dietary fiber: 0.6 g
Protein: 3 g

Health Benefit:
Healthy soy flour
is calcium rich.

ONION DILLY BREAD

Moist, fluffy, and onion-n-n-y good, this bread is a savory accompaniment to roast or chicken.

1/2 cup tofu, drained and mashed
1/4 cup warm tap water (110°F -115 °F)
2 tablespoons olive oil
3/4 cup low-fat cottage cheese
3/4 cup light sour cream
1 egg (room temperature)
3 1/3 cups bread flour
1/4 teaspoon baking soda
2 teaspoons salt
3 tablespoons granulated sugar
3 tablespoons minced dried onion
2 tablespoons dried dill
1 package active dry yeast

Select 2-pound loaf size. Add ingredients to bread machine in the above order. Select dough setting.

When dough cycle is complete, turn dough onto a floured surface. Dough will be wet and sticky. Gently work in flour until dough can be easily handled.

On cookie sheet coated with nonstick cooking spray, shape dough into two long loaves. Cover and let rise until doubled, about 1 1/2 hours.

Preheat oven to 350°F. Bake 15 to 18 minutes or until golden brown.

Yield: 15 slices

Do NOT use delayed timer for this recipe.

Your bread machine must have a dough setting to make this bread.

Nutrition Per Serving
Calories: 143.5
Total fat: 2.8 g
Cholesterol: 2 mg
Carbohydrates: 26 g
Dietary fiber: 1.1 g
Protein: 5.8 g

Health Benefit: Recent studies suggest that olive oil aids in the reduction of cardiovascular disease.

Notes

Those
Scrumptious
Breads

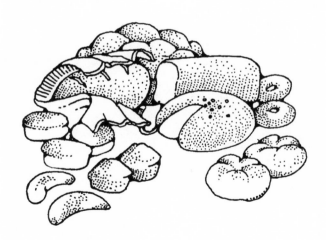

BREADS

Bread making began as an oral tradition, with recipes handed down from generation to generation. Early breads were naturally made with heart-healthy whole-grains. Rough peasant breads were chewy, thick crusted and seasoned with dried fruits and herbs.

The Egyptians were, perhaps, the first to flavor breads with sweet or aromatic herbs, enriching them with honey and eggs before shaping into loaves. Later, medieval bakers turned bread making into an art, fashioning breads to resemble birds, fish, and other animals. Each held a special symbolic meaning.

Bread still holds symbolic meaning. For many Christians, bread taken during communion, symbolizes the body of Christ. To Italians, bread remains a symbol of respect, even reverence. The French consider the perfect baguette and a good cheese a complete meal.

In many specialty shops, bread making has become an expression of culture, as rooted in history as are great works of art. Eating such bread can be like rediscovering an era gone by.

Worldwide, during feasts and holidays, bread celebrates the basic pleasure of living. The cook's basket of golden bread carries a blessing for those most revered in the home.

Fruits, vegetables, cheese, herbs, nuts, and spices add fragrance, color, and flavor to breads. Cooks, for centuries, have been dreaming up new and unusual ways to make a variety of crusty and chewy breads. With whole-grains becoming more popular in our society, breads are being restored to ancient taste. Genuine flavor once again enhances bread. Try adding savory basil, purple berries, scarlet apples, rich green olives, dark and sweet dates, or plump raisins to round, oblong, and braided breads. Let your imagination guide you as you experiment and create numerous textures and tastes.

To further increase flavor in breads for every meal, experiment with various types of grains. Such baking offers an excellent source of complex nutrients that can be found in no other foods on earth. Currently, whole-wheat flour, oat bran, and whole-grain oats are popular additions with American cooks. Yet, soy flour, quinoa, spelt, amaranth, and kamut can also bestow a harvest of varied taste, texture, and fragrance to every bread you serve. Since all of these flours offer dozens of known, and many possibly unknown nutrients, they should be included more often in everyday fare.

If your family prefers the look, taste, and texture of traditional white bread, you may need to introduce whole-grains slowly. Choose those that least affect taste and texture. Soy flour is perhaps the perfect way to sneak extra nourishment into traditional white bread without altering its appearance. When used as a partial substitute for all-purpose flour, you can make a high-rise white bread with excellent texture and flavor. If you don't tell your family of the substitution, they won't know you made it.

They won't know either about the increased iron, magnesium, calcium, zinc, vitamins, fiber, and phytochemicals that they're consuming—all nutrients the body craves and needs. When eating healthy foods, food cravings are soothed and hunger is pushed away. Because we are satisfied, we make fewer trips to the kitchen for leftover fried chicken, a peanut butter sandwich, or a bowl of chocolate ice cream.

GLUTEN MAKES BREAD RISE

Wheat comes in two varieties, hard and soft. Soft wheat is relatively low in gluten proteins. Hard varieties are gluten rich. Gluten makes bread rise and increases the protein content of baked goods. White and unbleached all-purpose flours contain both hard and soft wheat and are preferable for making yeast breads because of a higher gluten content. Whole-grain flours tend to be lower in gluten and need the addition of unbleached all-purpose flour to make breads and baked goods rise.

In most recipes, I use unbleached all-purpose flour as a base and incorporate smaller amounts of soy flour or other grains. Bread flour is high-gluten flour with 13-14 percent protein content and is recommended for most recipes using a bread machine. Vital gluten can be purchased in health food stores and most supermarket chains. Vital gluten makes higher volume bread.

SOY-ENRICHED BREAD

Other than protein and a few vitamins and minerals, bread made with refined white flour offers little nutritive value, unless the bread is fortified with powdered milk, yogurt, tofu, whole-grains, flaxseed meal, or other healthy nutrients. Breads made with even small additions of tofu and soy flour—both power-packed, energy-rich ingredients—have higher levels of complex nutrients the body needs.

Enriching bread at home is a simple task. In most bread recipes, you can easily replace one or two tablespoons of unbleached all-purpose flour with one or two tablespoons soy flour. Or, replace part of the shortening and eggs with one-quarter cup of tofu, thereby immediately improving the bread's nutritional quality.

To pump up nutrition, I often use four ounces or more of tofu in a bread recipe. Since tofu increases moistness in bread, it's difficult to overbake tofu-laced loaves. In early low-fat bread making experiments (without tofu), I often made dry, crusty, flavorless loaves of bread. With tofu and soy flour, my breads come out sweet smelling, moist, and fresh.

As a word of caution, remember to use lower fat soy products when making reduced-fat bread. I recommend using **low-fat silken tofu** with 1 percent fat per serving and defatted soy flour. The exception is in piecrust where a higher-fat soya powder is recommended. A truly tender piecrust simply needs the extra fat.

FORTIFYING BREAD

Since only wheat flour contains an appreciable amount of gluten, and gluten is necessary for an even rise in baked goods, it's necessary to first develop gluten before adding whole grains like wheat germ, cracked grains, soya powder, or soy flour. Soy flour contains no gluten, so it must be combined with wheat flour or other gluten-rich flours.

To develop gluten in wheat flour, use a mixer or food processor to thoroughly mix the dough before adding other desired grains. As a general rule of thumb, add gluten-rich flour to the first mixing. Then add lower gluten products, like wheat germ or soy flour, only after thoroughly beating the gluten and yeast.

BREAD TIPS

To make the best breads possible, follow these simple tips:

☐ To reduce fat content, coat pans with a nonstick cooking spray instead of greasing with butter, shortening, or oil.

☐ Always remove bread from baking pan, and let loaves cool on wire racks. Bread is best if sliced and served warm. To ensure even slices and few crumbs, use an electric knife.

☐ To store bread, cool it completely. Seal in plastic wrap and refrigerate.

Because dairy milk contains enzymes that make bread dough sticky, bring milk to the boiling point and cool to lukewarm before adding to bread mixture. Liquid that is too hot will kill the yeast. Since soy milk does not contain these enzymes, no heating is necessary.

GETTING STARTED

To make nourishing yeast bread, you need nothing more than flour, liquid, yeast, salt, oil, and tofu. Since kneading builds gluten in bread, it's important to knead bread thoroughly. Kneading by hand can take from 8 to 10 minutes. This time can be cut in half (or less) if using a dough-hook attachment on your mixer.

The bread-making process, on the whole, is simple. A basic bread is made using the following methods. Begin by dissolving yeast in warm water according to the recipe directions. In a food processor or with a mixer, blend sugar, salt, oil, tofu, milk, or other liquids called for in the recipe. Add wet ingredients to part of the unbleached all-purpose flour. Beat in other dry ingredients, including vital gluten to build gluten into the bread sponge. When gluten is well-developed, stir in whole-grain ingredients and as much of the remaining unbleached all-purpose flour as can be stirred in to make a stiff dough that pulls away from sides of bowl.

Most of this step will be by hand. Finally, turn dough onto a lightly floured surface and knead until smooth and elastic. Add just enough all-purpose flour to keep dough from sticking to work surface. Remember to avoid adding whole-grain flour during the kneading process.

Most yeast breads rise at least twice. Dough is placed in a large bowl coated with nonstick cooking spray. Dough is turned once to oil top. Cover bowl with a towel or plastic wrap. Allow dough to rise until double in bulk. Shape dough into loaves or rolls, cover them, and let rise a second time until double in bulk.

Warm temperatures stir yeast into action and help develop gluten, so bread rises best in a warm, draft-free place. Heat oven to a very low temperature, below 85° F. Turn it off. Make sure the oven stays well below 85° F . If dough gets too hot, the action of the yeast will be destroyed. The result—a flat, doughy mess.

TO SHAPE BREAD

While the shaping of bread can be considered an art for more intricate or elaborate creations, basic loaves follow just a few steps.

1. With a rolling pin or your hands, flatten dough to 15 x 7-inch oblong. Starting with the narrow end, roll the dough jellyroll fashion, sealing it at each turn with your fingertips or the edge of your hand.

2. Press down ends of loaf with the sides of your hands to make two thinly sealed strips. Fold these strips under loaf. Tuck loaf into a bread pan.

3. Cover and let rise in a warm place until doubled, about 1 to 2 hours. To test, press a fingertip gently into top of a loaf. If a dent remains, the dough is ready to bake.

4. When ready to bake, place loaf pans in middle of oven rack, leaving space between pans for heat to circulate. When bread has baked, test it by turning out one loaf and checking the bottom. The bottom should be golden brown and sound hollow when rapped with a finger.

5. Remove finished loaves from pans. Cool on a wire rack away from drafts. Slice with an electric knife. Serve warm.

TOFU AND BREAD DOUGH GO HAND-IN-HAND

Seldom thought of together, tofu and bread go hand-in-hand.

Tofu enhances dough and makes breads and other baked goods moist, rich, and tender. The texture of such breads is better quality than breads made without tofu.

Like soy flour, tofu is protein complementary. This means that protein from whole-grains, seeds, or nuts, combined with protein from tofu, is an effective protein that contains many of the essential amino acids the body needs.

Except for eggs, tofu is the only food that supplies all the necessary amino acids in adequate amounts.

SOY MILK IMPROVES DOUGH

Soy milk is an excellent alternative to dairy milk in any yeast bread recipe—and not just nutritionally. Soy milk improves the quality of bread dough by keeping bread tender. Many brands of low-fat soy milk are now readily available in supermarkets, health food stores, and specialty-food stores.

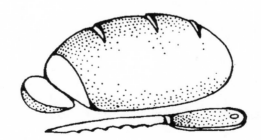

BASIC WHITE BREAD

Though this bread resembles and tastes much like the white bread Grandma used to make, this version is soy rich—and soy has never been so delicious.

1 package active dry yeast
1/4 cup warm water (110°F to 115°F)
3 tablespoons granulated sugar
2 teaspoons salt
1 tablespoon cooking oil
1/2 cup tofu, drained and mashed
2 cups nonfat milk, scalded and cooled
1/4 cup vital gluten
5 to 6 cups unbleached all-purpose flour

In large mixing bowl, dissolve yeast in warm water. Set aside.

Using a food processor or mixer, combine sugar, salt, oil, and tofu. Add to yeast. By hand, stir in milk, vital gluten, and 1 to 2 cups flour. Beat 1 to 2 minutes. Stir in enough remaining flour to make a stiff dough that pulls away from sides of bowl.

Turn dough onto a lightly floured surface. Knead until smooth and elastic, adding additional flour, if necessary.

Place dough in bowl coated with nonstick cooking spray, turning once to oil top. Cover and let rise in a warm place until doubled, about 1 to 2 hours.

Punch dough down and divide in half, shaping each half into a smooth ball. Cover and let rest 10 minutes. Place dough in two loaf pans coated with nonstick cooking spray. Cover and let rise in a warm place until doubled, about 1 hour.

Preheat oven to 350° F. Bake 30 minute or until top is golden brown. Remove loaves from pans. Cool on wire racks.

Yield: 24 slices

Nutrition Per Serving
Calories: 122
Total fat: 0.9
Dietary fiber: 0 .9 g
Cholesterol: 0
Carbohydrates: 23 g
Protein: 4.8 g

Health Benefit: Tofu adds protein, which is necessary for healthy hair, nails, and skin.

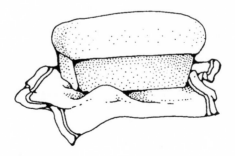

HEARTY WHOLE-WHEAT BREAD

Serve this hearty bread with honey and butter. What could be better on a cold winter day?

1 package active dry yeast
1/4 cup warm water (110°F to 115°F)
3 tablespoons granulated sugar
2 teaspoons salt
1 tablespoon cooking oil
1/2 cup tofu, drained and mashed
2 cups nonfat milk, scalded and cooled
1/2 cup vital gluten
3 to 4 cups unbleached all-purpose flour
2 cups whole-wheat flour

In large mixing bowl, dissolve yeast in water.

Using food processor or mixer, combine sugar, salt, oil, and tofu. Add to yeast mixture. Add milk, vital gluten, and 1 to 2 cups all-purpose flour. Beat 1 to 2 minutes. By hand, stir in whole-wheat flour and enough remaining all-purpose flour to make a stiff dough that pulls away from sides of bowl.

Turn dough onto a lightly floured surface. Knead until smooth and elastic, adding additional all-purpose flour, if necessary. Place dough in a bowl coated with nonstick cooking spray, turning once to oil top. Cover and let rise in a warm place until doubled, about 1 to 2 hours.

Punch dough down and divide in half, shaping each half into a smooth ball. Cover and let rest for 10 minutes. Place each ball in a loaf pan coated with nonstick cooking spray. Cover and let rise in a warm place until doubled, about 1 hour.

Preheat oven to 350°F. Bake 30 minutes or until top is golden brown. Remove loaves from pans. Cool on wire racks.

Yield: 24 slices

Nutrition Per Serving
Calories: 124
Total Fat: 1 g
Cholesterol: 0
Carbohydrates: 23 g
Dietary fiber: 1.8 g
Protein: 5.9 g

Health Benefits: Best known for a positive association with preventing heart disease, vitamin-E rich tofu has also been linked with many other health benefits, including strengthening the immune system.

HIGH-ENERGY SOY BREAD

Soy's goodness is so well-known today that this bread should be a favorite at any meal. This hearty, wholesome bread helps build strong bodies and provides the necessary energy to get through a busy day.

2 packages dry yeast
3 cups warm water (110°F to 115°F)
1/4 cup granulated sugar
1/2 cup tofu, drained and mashed
2 tablespoons cooking oil
3 teaspoons salt
1/2 cup vital gluten
5 to 6 cups unbleached all-purpose flour
1/2 cup soy flour

In large mixing bowl, dissolve yeast in water.

Using food processor or mixer, combine sugar, tofu, oil, and salt. Add to yeast mixture. By hand, stir in vital gluten and 2 to 3 cups all-purpose flour. Beat 2 to 3 minutes. Stir in soy flour. Add remaining all-purpose flour, 1 cup at a time, until dough is stiff and difficult to stir and pulls away from sides of bowl.

Place dough on a lightly floured surface . Knead until smooth and elastic, adding additional all-purpose flour, if necessary. Place dough in a bowl coated with nonstick cooking spray, turning once to oil top. Cover and let rise in warm place until doubled, about 1 to 2 hours.

Punch dough down and divide in half, shaping each half into a loaf. Place each in loaf pan coated with nonstick cooking spray. Cover and let rise in a warm place until doubled, about 1 to 2 hours.

Preheat oven to 325°F. Bake 50 to 55 minutes or until top is golden brown. Remove loaves from pans. Cool on wire racks.

Yield: 36 slices

Nutrition Per Serving
Calories: 104
Total fat: 1 g
Cholesterol: 0
Carbohydrates: 18 g
Dietary fiber: 1 g
Protein: 4 g

Health Benefits:
Soy bread is high in complex carbohydrates, potassium, folacin, and calcium, all necessary nutrients for strong muscles and bones.

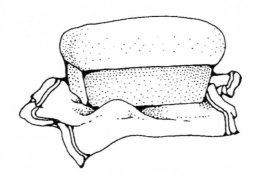

ROMAN MEAL MINI-LOAVES

Molasses, whole-grain flour, and soy make this bread healthy. You'll want to serve it often.

2 packages active dry yeast
1/2 cup warm water (110°F to 115°F)
1 cup rolled oats
2 3/4 cups boiling water
2 teaspoons salt
2 tablespoons cooking oil
1/2 cup blackstrap molasses
1/4 cup honey
1/2 cup tofu, drained and mashed
3 to 4 cups unbleached all-purpose flour
1 cup whole wheat flour
1/4 cup flaxseed meal

In large mixing bowl, dissolve yeast in warm water.

Add oats to the 2 3/4 cups boiling water. Let mixture cool to lukewarm. Using food processor or mixer, combine salt, oil, molasses, honey, and tofu. Add to cooled oat mixture.

Add cooled oat mixture to yeast mixture. By hand, stir in 1 to 2 cups of all-purpose flour. Beat on high speed of mixer 1 to 2 minutes. Add whole-wheat flour. Beat 1 to 2 additional minutes. By hand, stir in flaxseed meal and as much of the remaining all-purpose flour as is possible to make a dough that is sticky and pulls away from sides of bowl.

Turn dough onto a lightly floured surface. Knead 4 to 5 minutes, adding more all-purpose flour, if necessary, to keep dough from sticking to surface. Place dough in a bowl coated with nonstick cooking spray, turning once to oil top. Cover and let rise in a warm place until doubled, about 1 to 2 hours.

Punch dough down and divide among 8 mini-loaf pans coated with nonstick cooking spray. Cover and let rise in a warm place until doubled, about 1 hour.

Preheat oven to 350°F. Bake 25 to 30 minutes or until tops are golden brown. Remove from pans. Cool on wire racks.

Yield: 8 mini-loaves, 6 servings each

Nutrition Per Serving
Calories: 109
Total fat: 1.4 g
Cholesterol: 0
Carbohydrates: 20 g
Dietary fiber: 1 g
Protein: 4 g

Health Benefit: Flaxseed is heart healthy and has an estrogenic effect that some nutritionists suggest may aid in reducing menopause symptoms.

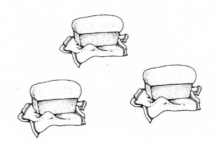

WHOLE-WHEAT FRENCH BREAD

Full of flavor and nutrition, this classic bread is fortified to make it healthy and tasty.

2 packages active dry yeast
3 cups warm water (110°F to 115°F)
1/4 cup tofu powder
4 teaspoons salt
2 cups whole-wheat flour
3 to 4 cups unbleached all-purpose flour
Olive oil (optional)
Minced garlic or garlic salt (optional)

In large mixing bowl, dissolve yeast in warm water. Stir in tofu powder, mixing with a wire whisk to dissolve. Stir in salt, whole-wheat flour, and 1 to 2 cups all-purpose flour. Beat 1 to 2 minutes on high. By hand, stir in enough remaining all-purpose flour to make a stiff dough that pulls away from sides of bowl.

Turn dough onto a floured surface. Let rest about 10 minutes. Knead 8 to 10 minutes, adding more all-purpose flour, if necessary, to keep the dough from sticking to surface. Dough should be smooth and full of bounce. As you knead, scrape up dough and slap it hard against the countertop. Repeat this process several times.

Put dough in a bowl coated with nonstick cooking spray, turning once to oil top. Cover with plastic wrap. Let dough stand in a warm place 3 to 4 hours. (Or cover bowl with plastic wrap and a plate to weigh down dough. Refrigerate overnight. Dough will triple in volume. When ready to use, remove plastic wrap. Let dough rise slowly in a warm place.)

Punch dough down. Cover and let rise again in warm place until doubled, about 1 to 2 hours. Punch down again. Turn onto a lightly floured surface. Divide dough into 6 equal parts. To form a loaf, place each part of dough on a lightly floured surface, patting to 14 x 15 inches. Fold lengthwise in thirds. With the side of your hand, firmly punch a lengthwise trough down the center and fold over, pinching edges together.

Coat baking sheet with nonstick cooking spray. Dust with cornmeal. Evenly space loaves on baking sheet. Brush tops lightly with olive oil, if desired, and sprinkle with minced garlic or garlic salt. Cover and let rise in a warm place until doubled, about 1 to 2 hours.

Preheat oven to 450°F. Bake 20 to 25 minutes or until crusty and golden brown.

Tip: French bread dough must be thoroughly kneaded and allowed to rise slowly.

Yield: 6 loaves (78 slices)

Nutrition Per Serving
Calories: 32
Total fat: 0.2 g
Cholesterol: 0
Carbohydrates: 6 g
Dietary fiber: 0.7 g
Protein: 1 g

Health Benefit: Tofu powder is packed with body-building protein.

ITALIAN HERB
CRESCENT ROLLS

Herbs add rich flavor and aroma to this familiar bread. Served with salad, soup, a buffet, or a meal, these rolls will always be welcomed by your family and guests.

DOUGH
1 package active dry yeast
1/4 cup warm water (110°F to 115°F)
3 tablespoons granulated sugar
2 teaspoons salt
1 tablespoon cooking oil
1/2 cup tofu, drained and mashed
2 cups nonfat milk, scalded and cooled
1/4 cup vital gluten
5 to 6 cups unbleached all-purpose flour

HERB COATING
3 tablespoons cooking oil
2 teaspoons parsley, minced
2 teaspoons oregano, minced
2 teaspoons thyme, minced
2 teaspoons basil, minced

In large mixing bowl, dissolve yeast in warm water.

Using a food processor or mixer, combine sugar, salt, oil, and tofu. Add to yeast. By hand, stir in milk, vital gluten, and 1 to 2 cups all-purpose flour. Beat 1 to 2 minutes. Stir in enough remaining flour to make a stiff dough that pulls away from sides of bowl.

Turn dough onto a lightly floured surface. Knead until smooth and elastic, adding more all-purpose flour, if necessary, to keep dough from sticking to surface. Place in a bowl coated with nonstick cooking spray, turning once to oil top. Cover and let rise in a warm place until doubled, about 1 to 2 hours.

Punch dough down. Divide into six parts. In a small mixing bowl, combine the herb-coating ingredients. Set aside.

Roll dough into 9-inch circles. Brush each with herb coating. Cut dough into 8 pie-shaped wedges.

Beginning with wide end, roll each wedge into a crescent. Arrange on cookie sheets coated with nonstick cooking spray. Cover and let rise in a warm place until doubled, about 1-2 hours.

Preheat oven to 350°F. Bake 20 to 25 minutes, or until tops are golden brown. Remove and let cool on wire racks.

Yield: 4 dozen rolls

Variation: Substitute 1 cup whole-wheat flour for 1 cup all-purpose flour.

Nutrition Per Serving
Calories: 125
Total fat: 2.4 g
Cholesterol: 0 mg
Carbohydrates: 25.5 g
Dietary fiber: 0.6 g
Protein: 2.8 g

Health Benefit: Herbs are nutritious additions to food. A tablespoon of basil contains 89 mg of calcium, and a tablespoon of oregano contains 71 mg of calcium. Basil is also rich in potassium and vitamin A.

YEAST BREADSTICKS

These breadsticks take a little time to make, but they're worth it. They have just the right crunchy texture for a simple or elegant Italian meal.

1 package active dry yeast
1 cup warm water (110°F to 115°F)
1/4 cup tofu, drained and mashed
2 tablespoons cooking oil
1 teaspoon salt
1/4 cup vital gluten
2 cups unbleached all-purpose flour
2 tablespoons soy flour

In large mixing bowl, dissolve yeast in warm water.

Using food processor or a mixer, combine tofu, oil, and salt. By hand, stir tofu mixture, vital gluten, and 1 cup all-purpose flour into yeast mixture. Beat 1 to 2 minutes. Stir in remaining all-purpose flour and soy flour to make a stiff dough.

Turn dough onto a lightly floured surface and knead 4 to 5 minutes, adding more all-purpose flour, if necessary, to make dough pliable and easy to handle.

Place dough in a bowl coated with nonstick cooking spray, turning once to oil top. Cover and let rise in warm place until doubled, about 1 to 2 hours. Punch dough down. On a floured surface, using rolling pin or hands, shape to 12 x 17-inch rectangle. Cover with plastic wrap and let rise until doubled, about 1 hour.

Cut dough in half, crosswise. Make 10 lengthwise cuts through each section of dough. Coat backs of two 12 x 17-inch baking sheets with nonstick cooking spray. Holding ends of each length of dough, pull and stretch to fit width of baking sheet. Lightly coat tops with olive oil. If desired, sprinkle with poppy seeds, wheat germ, or sesame seeds. Cover and let rise in a warm place about 15 minutes.

Preheat oven to 450°F. Bake 10 to 13 minutes, or until golden brown. Remove and cool on wire racks.

Yield: 20 breadsticks

Variations: *Whole-wheat breadsticks: Substitute 1 cup whole-wheat flour for 1 cup unbleached all-purpose flour.*

Garlic breadsticks: *Mince 1 clove of garlic and add to dough. Then sprinkle garlic powder and cooking oil over the unbaked tops. Yield: 20 breadsticks*

Nutrition Per Serving
Calories: 70
Total fat: 1.6 g
Cholesterol: 0
Carbohydrates: 10 g
Dietary fiber: 0.6 g
Protein: 3 g

Health Benefit:
Defatted soy flour provides a calcium boost to these breadsticks.

CINNAMON ROLLS

When you want a sweet treat, these are delicious.

2 packages active dry yeast
1 cup warm water (110°F to 115°F)
1 cup nonfat milk, scalded and cooled
1 1/2 teaspoons salt
1/2 cup sugar
2 tablespoons light butter
1 cup silken tofu, low-fat
1/4 cup vital gluten
6-7 cups unbleached all-purpose flour

FILLING:
4 tablespoons light butter
1 cup brown sugar, packed
4 teaspoons cinnamon

Spray four square pans or 2 oblong pans with nonstick cooking spray.

In large mixing bowl, dissolve yeast in warm water.

Scald milk by bringing it barely to a boil. Remove from heat. Cool to lukewarm. In food processor, using blade attachment, blend salt, sugar, butter, and tofu. Add this mixture to the yeast mixture. Add cooled milk.

By hand, stir in vital gluten and 1-2 cups all-purpose flour. Beat with mixer, 1-2 minutes. Stir in enough remaining all-purpose flour, one cup at a time, to make a stiff dough that is difficult to stir and pulls away from sides of bowl.

On lightly floured surface, knead dough 2-3 minutes or until smooth and elastic. Place in greased bowl, turning once to grease top. Cover with towel. Let rise in warm place until double, approximately 1- 2 hours.

Punch down. Divide dough into two pieces. On lightly floured surface, roll one piece into a 15 x 19-inch oblong. Mix brown sugar with the 4 teaspoons cinnamon. Spread dough with 2 tablespoons softened butter. Spread on 1/2 of the sugar and cinnamon mixture.

Roll dough up tightly, beginning at wide end. Seal edges by pinching together. Cut into 1-inch rolls. Place in prepared pans. Repeat process with second piece of dough. Cover rolls. Let rise in warm place that is free from drafts until double in bulk, 30-60 minutes.

Preheat oven to 350°F. Bake 25-30 minutes or until rolls begin to lightly brown on top. Remove from oven. Transfer to wire racks to cool. Spread glaze over tops, if desired.

GLAZE:
1 cup confectioners' sugar
2 teaspoons vanilla
4-6 teaspoons nonfat milk

Mix sugar, vanilla, and milk. Drizzle over rolls, if desired.

Yield: 38 rolls

Calories: 138
Total Fat: 2.1
Cholesterol: 5 mg
Carbohydrate: 28 g
Dietary fiber: .6 g
Protein: 3 g

Health Benefit: Tofu adds moisture to these rolls as well as protein and other important vitamins.

MUSHROOM-FILLED BREAD

Mushrooms fill every bite of this delicious bread

DOUGH
1 package active dry yeast
1 cup warm water (110°F to 115°F)
2 teaspoons molasses
1 1/2 teaspoons salt
1/2 teaspoon black pepper
2 tablespoons olive oil
1/2 cup tofu, drained and mashed
1/4 cup vital gluten
1 1/2 cups unbleached all-purpose flour
1/2 cup oat-bran flour

FILLING
3 tablespoons cooking oil
1/2 pound mushrooms, minced
2 tablespoons dried minced onion
1 teaspoon thyme
1/2 teaspoon black pepper
1 clove garlic, minced
1/2 cup softened reduced-fat or fat-free cream cheese

In large mixing bowl, dissolve yeast in warm water.

Using food processor or mixer, combine molasses, salt, pepper, cooking oil, and tofu. Add to yeast. By hand, stir in vital gluten and 1 to 2 cups all-purpose flour. Beat 1 to 2 minutes. Stir in oat-bran flour and enough all-purpose flour to make a stiff dough.

Turn dough onto a lightly floured surface. Knead 4 to 5 minutes or until smooth and elastic, adding more all-purpose flour, if necessary, to keep dough from sticking to surface. Place dough in a bowl coated with nonstick cooking spray, turning once to oil top. Cover and let rise in a warm place until doubled, about 1 to 2 hours.

Punch dough down and cut in half. On floured surface, roll one half to 11 x 17-inch rectangle. Roll second half to 8 x 13-inch rectangle. Place larger half on cookie sheet coated with nonstick cooking spray.

For filling, heat oil and sauté mushrooms, onion, thyme, pepper, and garlic 1 to 2 minutes. Spread softened cream cheese over larger half of dough. Top with mushroom mixture. Pull sides up about one-third of the way, leaving center open. Cut smaller half of dough into strips and crisscross. Cover and let rise in a warm place until puffy, about 30 minutes. Drizzle top lightly with olive oil.

Preheat oven to 350°F. Bake 20 to 25 minutes. Serve warm.

Yield: 17 servings

Nutrition Per Serving
Calories: 127
Total fat: 6 g
Cholesterol: 5 mg
Carbohydrates: 14 g
Dietary fiber: 1 g
Protein: 4 g

Health Benefit: Mushrooms contain traces of important B vitamins.

ITALIAN SPINACH ROLL

Spinach and cheese rolled up in a soy-laced bread makes a perfect vegetarian meal.

1 package active dry yeast
1/2 cup warm water (110°F to 115°F)
1 teaspoon molasses
3/4 teaspoon salt
1/4 teaspoon black pepper
1 tablespoon cooking oil
1/4 cup tofu, drained and mashed
2 tablespoons vital gluten
1 cup unbleached all-purpose flour
3 tablespoons oat-bran flour
1 cup grated fat-free mozzarella cheese
3/4 cup frozen chopped spinach, thawed
1/4 cup grated fat-free Parmesan cheese
1/2 teaspoon oregano
egg whites, for glaze

In large mixing bowl, dissolve yeast in warm water.

Using food processor or mixer, combine molasses, salt, pepper, cooking oil, and tofu. Add to yeast. By hand, stir in vital gluten and 3/4 cup all-purpose flour. Beat 1 to 2 minutes. Stir in bran flour and enough all-purpose flour to make a stiff dough that pulls away from sides of bowl and is difficult to stir.

Turn dough onto lightly floured surface. Knead 4 to 5 minutes or until smooth and elastic, adding more all-purpose flour, if necessary, to keep dough from sticking to surface. Place dough in a bowl coated with nonstick cooking spray, turning once to oil top. Cover and let it rise in warm place until double in bulk, about 1 to 2 hours.

Coat baking sheet with nonstick cooking spray. Punch dough down. Roll on floured surface to a 10 x 12-inch rectangle. Place on prepared baking sheet. Spread half of mozzarella cheese over center third of rectangle. Squeeze excess water from spinach. Combine spinach, Parmesan cheese, and oregano. Spread mixture over mozzarella. Top with remaining mozzarella.

Using a sharp knife, make slits at 1-inch intervals from edges of the filling-covered portion to the top and bottom edges of dough. Alternating from either end, fold strips at an angle over filling area. Cover. Allow dough to rise in a warm place until doubled, about 30 minutes. Brush top with an egg-white glaze.

Preheat oven to 350°F. Bake 25 minutes or until golden brown.

Yield: 12 slices

Nutrition Per Serving
Calories: 95
Total fat: 2 g
Cholesterol: 3 mg
Carbohydrates: 12 g
Dietary fiber: 1 g
Protein: 7 g

Health Benefit: A one-cup serving of spinach contains no cholesterol and only 0.1 g of fat. It has a whopping 2,707 IU of vitamin A, 40 mg of calcium, and 78.4 mcg of folacin as well as other important nutrients.

WHEAT-N-CARROT ROLLS

This tender, rich, golden bread adds a festive touch to a Thanksgiving table or buffet. It is a vegan recipe that will please everyone.

1 package active dry yeast
1 1/2 cups warm water (110°F to 115°F)
1/2 cup tofu, drained and mashed
2 tablespoons olive oil
1 jar (4 ounces) baby food carrots
1/4 cup maple syrup
1 teaspoon salt
1/4 cup vital gluten
4 cups unbleached all-purpose flour
1 cup whole-wheat flour
2 tablespoons soy flour

In large mixing bowl, dissolve yeast in warm water.

Using food processor or mixer, combine tofu, olive oil, baby food, syrup, and salt. Add to yeast. By hand, stir in vital gluten and 3 cups all-purpose flour. Beat 1 to 2 minutes. Add whole-wheat flour and continue beating 1 to 2 minutes. Add soy flour, plus enough remaining all-purpose flour to form stiff dough that pulls away from sides of the bowl and is difficult to stir.

Turn dough onto a lightly floured surface. Knead 4 to 5 minutes, adding more all-purpose flour, if necessary, to keep dough from sticking to surface. Place dough in a bowl coated with nonstick cooking spray, turning once to oil top. Cover and let rise in warm place, about 1 to 2 hours.

Punch dough down. Shape into rolls. Place on greased baking sheet. Cover. Let rise in warm place free from drafts, approximately 1 hour.

Preheat oven to 350°F. Bake 20-25 minutes or until golden brown. Remove and cool on a wire rack.

Yield: 20 servings

This is a vegan recipe

Nutrition Per Serving
Calories: 99
Total fat: 1.3 g
Cholesterol: 0
Carbohydrates: 18 g
Dietary fiber: 1 g
Protein: 3.7 g

Health Benefit: Carrots are rich in beta-carotene, which is attributed to helping fight free radicals in the body.

Notes

Quick & Easy Breads

QUICK BREADS

Quick breads—which are made without yeast and rise due to the action of baking powder, baking soda, or just steam—are a great way to add nutrition and taste to your diet. Besides tofu and soy flour, many recipes in *Beyond Low-Fat Baking* include fresh fruit—an excellent way to slip those 5-A day fruits and vegetables into the diet.

Pineapple, bananas, apricots, apples, oranges, cranberries, or blueberries are just a few of the tasty fruits that enhance flavor, increase sweetness, provide delightful bursts of color, and are antioxidant and photochemical-rich. Research also indicates that long-time favorite baking ingredients, such as lemon and orange zest, boost taste and may be super packed with cancer-fighting chemicals. Just don't over do. While orange and lemon peel are healthy, excessive amounts of citrus peel may have harmful effects.

Some quick bread recipes use dried fruits rather than fresh. Dried fruits store easily and are convenient. Apples, dates, cherries, apricots, peaches, and bananas are among the many readily available dried fruits. Dried fruits, like all fruits, offer powerful antioxidant properties.

Other recipes call for fruit-juice concentrate to provide a natural sweetness and reduce sugar used in a recipe. Be careful when incorporating fruit juice concentrate. Too much causes quick breads or muffins to easily burn.

CONCERNING EGG SUBSTITUTES

Sometimes, I use egg substitutes in baking. It is true that cholesterol and fat free egg substitutes are appealing, but egg substitutes contain coloring agents, thickeners, and preservatives. Check labels carefully. As a general guideline, use egg substitutes only when a recipe calls for a large number of eggs. Otherwise, use egg whites in place of part or all of the whole eggs.

Egg substitutes tend to produce tougher-textured muffins and quick breads. To keep texture tender and light, a whole egg can be included along with egg whites. Whole eggs do contain cholesterol and may need to be avoided by individuals following a doctor-prescribed cholesterol-lowering diet. But for those on a regular diet, eggs are usually allowed in moderation.

Although of animal origin, and not recommended in large quantities, whole eggs are a rich source of protein. Even though a whole egg contains 5 grams of fat, when divided among 12 muffins, the per muffin increase in fat content is low.

AVOID FAT FREE MARGARINES

As a rule, I never use fat-free margarine in quick breads or any baking, for that matter. I find fat-free margarine has an objectionable taste and lacks flavor. Numerous cookbooks tout these products, but I have tried them in dozens of muffins and other quick breads and have yet to find one that produced a high-quality baked good that retained either flavor or texture. Fat-free margarine is watery and simply doesn't contain the necessary ingredients to keep quick breads tender.

A better alternative is **low-fat silken tofu**, which contains 1 percent fat per serving. As a substitute, low-fat tofu allows for a considerable reduction in fat and creates tender, flavorful quick bread. Utilizing mashed or pureed fruits or baby food reduces fat content even more.

SHOULD YOU USE NUTS?

Some recipes in this book call for nuts as optional ingredients. You (and your doctor, if you are under a physician's care) must decide whether to include nuts in your diet. Nuts of all sorts are getting attention from health-care specialists these days simply because nuts are powerhouses of a vast array of nutrients.

Nuts are, of course, high in calories and fat. One cup contains about 800 calories and 70 grams of fat. They are best served in very small portions. On the plus side, nuts provide the essential fats the body needs daily, and they are one of the few unprocessed foods we eat with any regularity. Since unprocessed foods contain both known and unknown nutrients, and the American Cancer Association recommends eating a wide variety of foods, nuts of all sorts, if eaten in moderation, can increase over all nutrition.

The fat in many nuts is unsaturated and does not raise blood cholesterol levels. Like tofu, nuts provide important minerals, such as magnesium, zinc, copper, plus vitamin E. Familiarize yourself with a variety of nuts. Many cooks include walnuts or pecans in baked goods, but filberts or Brazil nuts contain the richest sources of selenium, a mineral that many health authorities suggest is a good cancer preventive. Almonds are isoflavone rich.

QUICK BREAD TIPS

Incorporate these tips into your quick bread creations, and you're assured of success.

■ Stir the batter as little as possible. If batter is overmixed, the result will be tough quick breads.

■ Combine all dry ingredients in one bowl. Measure and combine dry ingredients before sifting them. Sifting is especially important with ingredients like soy flour (if it contains lumps from being refrigerated), baking soda, and baking powder.

■ Make sure baking powder and baking soda are fresh. Check the package dates. If old, discard them.

■ Always beat wet ingredients separately from dry ingredients. Then stir wet ingredients into the dry, blending just until moistened. Finally, fold in nuts or fruits.

■ To reduce fat, coat baking pans and baking sheets with

nonstick cooking spray.

■ For best results, eat quick breads the day they are made. After twenty-four hours, refrigerate leftovers. Never store them in hot or humid rooms since any quick bread will mold under such conditions.

■ Quick breads made with tofu will mold before they will dry out. After a day or two, you may want to discard remaining portions.

PREPACKAGED MIXES

Tofu's health benefits can quickly be added to prepackaged muffin, cornbread, or cake mixes. Simply use a mixer to make tofu creamy before adding it to the prepackaged mix. Then proceed with package directions. Any beadiness in the mixture will dissolve in the baking process.

BISCUITS, PANCAKES, AND WAFFLES

Family favorites--biscuits, pancakes, and waffles--can be healthful dietary choices if made with additions of whole foods, such as tofu. Yet, when whole-grains, such as amaranth flour, flaxseed meal, and whole-grain cornmeal, are combined with soy, you and your family are assured of getting a wider range of nutrients. For flavor and nutrition, dress up pancakes and waffles with strawberries, blackberries, blueberries, kiwi, yogurt, walnuts, raisins or any combination of nuts and fruits. Try a variety of flavorful syrups for unexpected taste sensations.

BANANA NUT BREAD

Full of rich banana flavor, this moist bread is perfect for break-fast or brunch any day of the year.

1 1/4 cups unbleached all-purpose flour
1/4 cup soy flour
3/4 teaspoon baking soda
1 teaspoon baking powder
1/2 teaspoon salt
2 egg whites
3 tablespoons cooking oil
1 cup granulated sugar
5 bananas, mashed
1 teaspoon vanilla
1/2 cup walnuts (optional)

Preheat oven to 350°F. Combine all-purpose flour, soy flour, baking soda, baking powder, and salt. Set aside. In separate bowl, using medium speed of mixer, beat egg whites, oil, sugar, bananas, and vanilla. By hand, stir wet ingredients into dry. Blend just until mixed. Do not overstir. Stir in walnuts.

Coat 1 loaf pan with nonstick cooking spray. Pour batter into pan. Bake 45 to 55 minutes or until a toothpick inserted into center comes out clean. Cool in pans. Remove to a wire rack.

Yield: 12 servings

Nutrition Per Serving
Calories: 181
Total fat: 3.7 g
Cholesterol: 0
Carbohydrates: 35 g
Dietary fiber: 1 g
Protein: 3.2 g

Health Benefit: Bananas-- which replace part of the fat in this lower fat recipe--contain 1.8 g of fiber, 293 mg of potassium, 60 IU of vitamin A, and 7 mg of vitamin C.

SUNBURST CRANBERRY BREAD

A whole orange gives this bread a wonderful full-bodied taste and leaves your kitchen smelling oh so good.

1 1/4 cups unbleached all-purpose flour
2 tablespoons soy flour
1 1/4 cups brown sugar, packed
2 teaspoons baking powder
1/2 teaspoon baking soda
1/2 teaspoon salt
2 tablespoons cooking oil
3 egg whites
1/2 cup tofu, drained and mashed
2 tablespoons baby food prunes, 2 1/2 ounces
1-2 oranges, washed and seeded, reserving peel
1 cup chopped dried cranberries

Preheat oven to 350°F.

Combine all-purpose flour, soy flour, brown sugar, baking powder, baking soda, and salt.

In separate bowl, using medium speed of mixer, beat oil, egg whites, tofu, and baby food prunes. By hand, stir wet ingredients into dry ingredients. Blend just until mixed. Do not overstir.

In a food processor or blender, puree the oranges. Grate peeling. Measure 1 cup orange pulp and add to batter. Stir in orange peel and cranberries, mixing just until moistened. Coat loaf pan with nonstick cooking spray. Spoon in batter.

Bake 45 to 55 minutes or until a toothpick inserted into center comes out clean. Cool in pan. Remove to a wire rack.

Yield: 15 servings

Nutrition Per Serving
Calories: 140
Total fat: 2 g
Cholesterol: 0
Carbohydrates: 28 g
Dietary fiber: 0.9 g
Protein: 3 g

Health Benefit: Oranges contain dietary fiber and calcium. Each 3/4-cup serving of fresh oranges contain 254 mg of potassium, 91 mg of calcium, 1 mg of iron, 0.1 mg of zinc, 324 IU of vitamin A, 0.12 mg of vitamin B6, 0.13 mg of vitamin B1, 0.06 mg of vitamin B2, 38.9 mcg of folacin, and 0.7 mg of niacin.

LEMON TEA BREAD

Not too sweet yet perfectly flavored, this bread is moist and delicious.

1/4 cup whole-wheat flour
1 3/4 cups unbleached all-purpose flour
3 tablespoons soy flour
1 1/4 cups granulated sugar
2 teaspoons baking powder
1/2 teaspoon baking soda
1/2 teaspoon salt
1/2 cup tofu, drained and mashed
2 tablespoons baby food prunes, 2 1/2 ounces
2 tablespoons cooking oil
3 egg whites
1-2 lemons, washed and seeded, retaining peel
1/4 cup water
1/4 cup golden raisins

Preheat oven to 350°F.

Combine whole-wheat flour, all-purpose flour, soy flour, sugar, baking powder, baking soda, and salt.

In separate bowl, using medium speed of mixer, beat tofu, baby food prunes, oil and egg whites. By hand, stir wet ingredients into dry. Blend just until mixed. Do not overstir.

In food processor or blender, puree lemon. Grate peel. Add 1/2 cup lemon pulp to batter. Stir in water, grated lemon peel, and raisins, mixing on low speed of mixer just until ingredients are moistened. Coat loaf pan with nonstick cooking spray. Spoon in batter.

Bake 60 to 65 minutes or until a toothpick inserted into center comes out clean. Cool in pan. Remove to a wire rack.

Yield: 15 servings

Nutrition Per Serving
Calories: 163
Total fat: 2 g
Cholesterol: 0
Carbohydrates: 33 g
Dietary fiber: 1 g
Protein: 4 g

Health Benefit: Good sources of vitamin C, lemons also contain fiber and B vitamins.

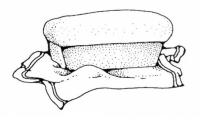

MUFFINS

Muffins take little time to prepare, and today's low-fat or fat-free muffins are both healthy and delicious. Muffins are an easy way to get complex carbohydrates. They are a high energy mid-afternoon pick-me-up or a satisfying snack at the end of the day.

MUFFINS FROM MIXES

While muffins are easy to make from scratch, many cooks prefer mixes, so I have included ways to add soy to prepackaged muffin mixes. I haven't tested every brand of mix, but those that I have tried worked beautifully. (I generally buy either brand-name mixes or whole-grain ones from natural food stores.) Experiment for yourself. You can easily give your family the benefit of soy, even when you have little time to bake.

When working with muffin mixes, I have found that I can generally follow the instructions on the box and simply add up to a half-cup of mashed tofu with other liquids from the recipe. Tofu is not used as a partial fat substitute but is used as a nutritious addition to these easy to make treats. Use the oven temperature and cooking time called for on the mix. *Tip: Muffins with tofu added do not brown as much, so don't wait for muffins to get as dark on the top. To check, insert a toothpick into center. If it comes out clean, muffins are finished baking.*

MUFFIN TIPS

Certain rules should always be followed for making perfect muffins.

■ Make only one batch of muffins at a time. (The exception in this book is Refrigerator Bran Muffins.) Most muffin recipes must be stirred with care, and large batches can be problematic since they are generally overmixed.

■ When filling cups with batter, it's generally best to fill them three-quarters full for lower fat muffins.

■ As with all baking, correct oven temperature is essential for muffins. Preheat oven, and avoid putting the batter in until the exact temperature is reached. When the temperature is too low, muffins will be flat or sink in the middle. A too-hot oven will cause uneven peaks. It is best to only bake 6 to 12 muffins at a time. If your recipe makes more than a dozen muffins, bake them separately.

■ To check to see if muffins are done, stick a toothpick into the center, and when it comes out clean, the muffins are finished baking. Be sure to cool muffins 10 minutes before removing from cups. Hot muffins tend to collapse. Finish cooling them on wire racks.

■ Muffins made with tofu need to be refrigerated after a day. Never store muffins or quick breads in a hot room since humidity will cause products to mold.

CRANBERRY PINEAPPLE MUFFINS

The combination of cranberries and pineapple has always been a hit. This muffin is great for lunch boxes or after-school snacks.

1 cup unbleached all-purpose flour
1/2 cup soy flour
2 teaspoons baking powder
1/2 teaspoon baking soda
1/2 teaspoon salt
1/2 teaspoon cinnamon
1/4 cup cooking oil
1 cup brown sugar, packed
3 egg whites
1/2 cup applesauce
1 teaspoon vanilla extract
3/4 cup cranberries
1/2 cup chopped dried pineapple
1/4 cup chopped walnuts (optional)

Preheat oven to 350°F. Wash and sort cranberries. Chop coarsely.

In medium bowl, combine all-purpose flour, soy flour, baking powder, baking soda, salt, and cinnamon. In separate bowl, beat oil, sugar, egg whites, applesauce, and vanilla. Stir wet ingredients into dry and blend just until mixed. Do not overstir. Add cranberries, pineapple, and walnuts.

Coat muffin tins with nonstick cooking spray. Spoon in batter, filling each cup three-quarters full. Bake 20-22 minutes or until a toothpick inserted into center comes out clean. Let muffins cool in tins 10 minutes. Remove to a wire rack to finish cooling.

Yield: 12 muffins

Nutrition Per Serving
Calories: 200
Total fat: 4.9 g
Cholesterol: 0
Carbohydrates: 36 g
Dietary fiber: 2 g
Protein: 4 g

Health Benefit:
Cranberries contain 74 mg of potassium, 7 mg of calcium, and traces of iron, zinc, B vitamins, and folacin in each one-cup serving.

LEMON-POPPY SEED MUFFINS

While a little higher in fat, these muffins are drastically reduced from the original version.

1 cup unbleached all-purpose flour
1/3 cup soy flour
1/2 teaspoon baking soda
1 teaspoon baking powder
1/4 teaspoon salt
1 1/3 cups granulated sugar
1/4 cup light sour cream
1/4 cup tofu, drained and mashed
1/4 cup cooking oil
3 egg whites
1/4 cup lemon juice
1 teaspoon grated lemon peel
1 teaspoon vanilla
3 tablespoons poppy seeds

Preheat oven to 375°F. In medium bowl, combine all-purpose flour, soy flour, baking soda, baking powder, and salt. Set aside. In separate bowl, mix sugar, sour cream, tofu, oil, egg whites, and lemon juice. Stir wet ingredients into dry, blending just until mixed. Do not overstir. Add lemon peel, vanilla, and poppy seeds. Coat muffin tins with nonstick cooking spray. Spoon in batter, filling each cup three-quarters full. Bake 25 to 30 minutes or until a toothpick inserted into the center comes out clean. Cool in tins 10 minutes. Remove to a wire rack.
Yield: 12 muffins

Nutrition Per Serving
Calories: 202
Total fat: 8.1 g
Cholesterol: 2 mg
Carbohydrates: 33 g
Dietary fiber: 1.1 g
Protein: 4.4 g

Health Benefit: One lemon contains 336 mg of potassium and 70 IU of vitamin A.

GLORIOUS GINGER MUFFINS

Full of ginger, these muffins smell heavenly and taste absolutely sinful. They're a great mid-morning energy pick-me-up.

1 3/4 cups unbleached all-purpose flour
1/4 cup soy flour
1/2 teaspoon salt
3/4 teaspoon baking soda
1 teaspoon baking powder
1 cup granulated sugar
1/4 cup brown sugar, packed
3 tablespoons cooking oil
3 egg whites
1 cup low-fat buttermilk
2 tablespoons grated fresh gingerroot
2 tablespoons lemon zest

Preheat oven to 375°F. In medium bowl, combine all-purpose flour, soy flour, salt, baking soda, baking powder, granulated sugar, and brown sugar. Set aside. In separate bowl, mix oil, egg whites, and buttermilk. Stir wet ingredients into dry, blending just until mixed. Do not overstir. Add gingerroot and lemon zest.

Coat muffin tins with nonstick cooking spray. Spoon in batter, filling each cup three-quarters full. Bake 20 to 25 minutes or until toothpick inserted into the center comes out clean. Let muffins cool in tins 10 minutes. Remove to wire racks.
Yield: 12 muffins

Nutrition Per Serving
Calories: 195
Total fat: 3.8 g
Cholesterol: 1 mg
Carbohydrates: 37.1 g
Dietary fiber: 0.7 g
Protein: 3.6 g

Health Benefit: A tablespoon of ginger contains 73 mg of potassium, 6 mg of calcium, and traces of iron.

REFRIGERATOR BRAN MUFFINS

When planning for a crowd, these muffins are perfect since you can make the batter ahead of time, keep it in the refrigerator, and simply bake when needed.

4½ cups raisin bran cereal
1 teaspoon baking soda
1½ cups granulated sugar
2 cups unbleached all-purpose flour
½ cup soy flour
1 teaspoon salt
2 egg whites
1 egg
½ cup oil
2 cups buttermilk, low-fat

Preheat oven to 400°F. In large bowl, combine cereal, baking soda, sugar, all-purpose flour, soy flour, and salt. Set aside. In separate bowl, beat egg whites, egg, oil, and buttermilk. Stir wet ingredients into dry. Blend just until mixed. Do not overstir.

Coat muffin tin with nonstick cooking spray. Spoon in batter, filling each cup three-quarters full. Bake 20 minutes or until toothpick inserted into center comes out clean. Let muffins cool in tins 10 minutes. Remove to a wire rack.
Store the remaining batter in an airtight container in refrigerator
Yield: 24 muffins

Nutrition Per Serving
Calories: 147
Total fat: 4.3 g
Cholesterol: 1 mg
Carbohydrates: 25 g
Dietary fiber: 1.2 g
Protein: 3.4 g

Health Benefit: Cereal is part of a complex carbohydrate diet, which the USDA recommends for healthful eating.

DEVIL'S FOOD MUFFINS

If you like chocolate, you'll love these muffins. Drizzle them with a chocolate glaze or your favorite chocolate frosting for an added treat.

2 cups unbleached all-purpose flour
¼ cup soy flour
¼ teaspoon salt
¾ teaspoon baking soda
1 teaspoon baking powder
1 cup granulated sugar
3 tablespoons cooking oil
3 egg whites
1 cup low-fat buttermilk
½ cup chocolate syrup
1 teaspoon vanilla

Preheat oven to 400°F. In large mixing bowl, combine all-purpose flour, soy flour, salt, baking soda, baking powder, and sugar. Set aside. In separate bowl, beat oil, egg whites, and buttermilk. Stir wet ingredients into dry. Blend until just mixed. Do not overstir. Add chocolate syrup and vanilla.

Coat muffin tin with nonstick cooking spray. Spoon in batter, filling each cup three-quarters full. Bake 15 to 20 minutes or until toothpick inserted into center comes out clean. Let muffins cool in tins 10 minutes. Remove to a wire rack. When cool, frost with your favorite chocolate icing, if desired.

Yield: 12 muffins

Nutrition Per Serving
Calories: 218
Total fat: 4.0 g
Cholesterol: 1 mg
Carbohydrates: 42 g
Dietary fiber: 0.9 g
Protein: 4.9 g

Health Benefit: Soy flour adds calcium and B vitamins to these delicious muffins.

BEST BANANA MUFFINS

These muffins are moist and banana-y-licious.

1 1/4 cups unbleached all-purpose flour
1/4 cup soy flour
3/4 teaspoon baking soda
1 teaspoon baking powder
1/4 teaspoon salt
2 egg whites
3 tablespoons cooking oil
1 cup granulated sugar
5 bananas, mashed
1 teaspoon vanilla
1/2 cup walnuts (optional)

Preheat oven to 350°F.

In medium bowl, combine all-purpose flour, soy flour, baking soda, baking powder, and salt. Set aside. In separate bowl, beat egg whites, oil, and sugar. Fold in bananas and vanilla. Stir wet ingredients into dry. Blend just until mixed. Do not overstir. Add walnuts.

Coat muffin tin with nonstick cooking spray. Spoon in batter, filling each cup three-quarters full. Bake 18 to 22 minutes or until toothpick inserted into center comes out clean. Let muffins cool in tins 10 minutes. Remove to a wire rack.

Yield: 12 muffins

Nutrition Per Serving
Calories: 181
Total fat: 3.7 g
Cholesterol: 0
Carbohydrates: 35 g
Dietary fiber: 1 g
Protein: 3.2 g

Health Benefit: A banana is a nearly perfect food. One medium banana contains 293 mg of potassium. It is often called the potassium bomb.

STRAWBERRY-LEMON MUFFINS

Lemon and strawberry are a winning combination.

1 cup unbleached all-purpose flour
1/3 cup soy flour
1/2 teaspoon baking soda
1 teaspoon baking powder
1/4 teaspoon salt
1/4 cup nonfat milk
1 1/3 cups granulated sugar
1/4 cup tofu, drained and mashed
1/4 cup light sour cream
3 tablespoons cooking oil
3 egg whites
1 teaspoon vanilla
2 teaspoons lemon zest
3/4 cup diced strawberries

Preheat oven to 375°F. In medium bowl, combine all-purpose flour, soy flour, baking soda, baking powder, and salt. Set aside. In separate bowl, beat milk, sugar, tofu, sour cream, cooking oil, and egg whites. Add vanilla. Stir wet ingredients into dry. Blend just until mixed. Do not overstir. Add lemon zest and strawberries. Coat muffin tin with nonstick cooking spray. Spoon in batter, filling each cup three-quarters full. Bake 20 to 25 minutes or until toothpick inserted into the center comes out clean. Let muffins cool in tins 10 minutes. Remove to wire racks.
Yield: 12 muffins

Nutrition Per Serving
Calories: 184
Total fat: 6.1 g
Cholesterol: 2 mg.
Carbohydrates: 33 mg.
Dietary fiber: 0.6 g
Protein: 4.2 g

H e a l t h B e n e f i t :
Strawberies top the list for antioxidant benefits.

PINEAPPLE CARROT MUFFINS

What a wonderful way to eat your carrots and satisfy a sweet tooth at the same time. These luscious, moist muffins are the best tasting ever and healthful enough to serve every day.

1/2 cup whole-wheat flour
1/4 cup soy flour
1 3/4 cups unbleached all-purpose flour
1/2 cup granulated sugar
1/2 cup brown sugar, packed
1/2 teaspoon baking soda
1 teaspoon baking powder
1/4 teaspoon salt
1 1/2 cups nonfat milk
2 egg whites
2 tablespoons cooking oil
3/4 cup crushed pineapple, drained
1/2 cup grated carrots
2 tablespoons grated gingerroot

Preheat oven to 400°F.

In medium mixing bowl, combine whole-wheat flour, soy flour, all-purpose flour, granulated sugar, brown sugar, baking soda, baking powder, and salt.

In separate bowl, beat milk, egg whites, and oil. Stir wet ingredients into dry. Blend just until mixed. Do not overstir. Add pineapple, carrots, and gingerroot.

Coat muffin tin with nonstick cooking spray. Spoon in batter, filling each cup three-quarters full. Bake 15 to 20 minutes or until toothpick inserted in center comes out clean. Let muffins cool in tins 10 minutes. Remove to a wire rack.

Yield: 18 muffins

Nutrition Per Serving
Calories: 203
Total fat: 2.7 g
Cholesterol: 1 mg
Carbohydrates: 40 g
Dietary fiber: 1.5 g
Protein: 5.3 g

Health Benefit: Carrots are rich in vitamin A, with one cup containing a whopping 27,519 IU of this important vitamin. They also offer 316 mg of potassium, 26 mg of calcium, 13.7 mcg of folacin, and traces of iron and zinc.

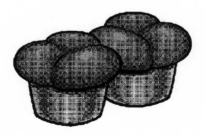

BLUEBERRY BREAKFAST SQUARES

At the test kitchen, we wanted to include prepackages mixes to show how easily soy can be slipped into ordinary foods.

1 box (16.5 ounces) fat-free blueberry muffin mix with canned blueberries
1/2 cup light sour cream
3/4 cup nonfat milk
2 egg whites
1/2 cup tofu, drained and mashed
1/2 cup brown sugar, packed
1/4 teaspoon grated orange peel

Preheat oven to 350°F. Coat 9 x 13-inch pan with nonstick cooking spray.

Spread canned blueberries in bottom of prepared pan. Top with sour cream.

In medium bowl, combine dry muffin mix with milk, egg whites, and tofu, stirring until dry ingredients are moistened and tofu is blended. Pour mixture over sour cream layer. In small bowl, combine brown sugar and orange peel. Spread over top. Swirl through batter with a knife.

Bake 20 to 22 minutes. Cut into squares and serve warm.

Yield: 12 servings

Nutrition Per Serving
Calories: 62
Total fat: 0.3 g
Cholesterol: 1 mg
Carbohydrates: 13 g
Dietary fiber: 0.2 g
Protein: 2 g

Health Benefit:
Potassium-rich blueberries also contain 9.1 mcg of folacin per one-cup serving.

BLUEBERRY MUFFINS

Full of luscious blueberries, these muffins are wonderfully sweet.

1 1/2 cups unbleached all-purpose flour
1/4 cup soy flour
1 teaspoon baking powder
1 teaspoon baking soda
1/4 teaspoon salt
1/4 teaspoon lemon juice
1 cup granulated sugar
1/4 cup cooking oil
1 egg
2 egg whites
3/4 cup buttermilk, low-fat
3/4 cup frozen blueberries

Preheat oven to 375°F.

In medium bowl, combine all-purpose flour, soy flour, baking powder, baking soda, and salt. Set aside. In separate bowl, beat lemon juice, sugar, oil, egg, egg whites, and buttermilk until light and fluffy. Stir wet ingredients into dry. Blend until just mixed. Do not overstir. Gently fold in blueberries.

Coat muffin tin with nonstick cooking spray. Spoon in batter, filling each cup three-quarters full. Bake 18 to 23 minutes or until toothpick inserted into center comes out clean. Let muffins cool in tins 10 minutes. Remove to a wire rack.
Yield: 12 muffins

Nutrition Per Serving
Calories: 182
Total fat: 4.9
Cholesterol: 1 mg
Carbohydrates: 31.5 g
Dietary fiber: 0.8 g
Protein: 3.7 g

Health Benefit: This winning combination of blueberries and lemon provides these muffins with a real potassium boost, while soy flour adds calcium and a host of B vitamins.

BANANA MUFFINS FROM A MIX

Made from a prepackaged mix, these soy-laced muffins are easy, quick, and nutritious.

1/2 cup tofu, drained and mashed
1 cup water
1 box (14 ounces) fat-free banana muffin mix

Preheat oven to 400°F.

In medium bowl, combine dry muffin mix, tofu, and water, stirring just until tofu is blended and ingredients are combined. Do not overstir.

Coat muffin tin with nonstick cooking spray. Spoon in batter, filling each cup three-quarters full. Bake 16 to 18 minutes or until toothpick inserted into center comes out clean. Let muffins cool in tins 10 minutes. Remove to a wire rack.

Yield: 12 muffins

Variation: *Any flavor of muffin mix can be used.*

Nutrition Per Serving
Calories: 120
Total fat: 0.2 g
Cholesterol: 0
Carbohydrates: 28.3 g
Dietary fiber: 1.7 g
Protein: 2.5 g

Health Benefit: Besides potassium, one banana contains 14.1 mcg of folacin and traces of B vitamins.

Biscuits & Scones

SCONES & BISCUITS

Scones are so easy to make and fun to serve. These quick and easy breads are an American favorite and can easily be included in a heart-healthy diet.

When made with cooking oil and the healthful properties of tofu and soy flour, these tender scones provide important nutrients the body needs. These recipes use low-fat buttermilk and soy milk, both good sources of calcium. To use tofu in scones, the tofu must be creamy enough to blend with other ingredients. A food processor or blender will make this process quick and easy. **Use only low-fat silken tofu, 1% fat per serving.**

Biscuits, like scones, can be heathier with tofu or soy flour added to them while retaining that light, tender, melt-in-your mouth goodness we expect from such food. Vegetables, such as the sweet potato, are easily added to biscuits. In addition to adding fiber to the diet, sweet potatos are high in vitamin A and numerous other nutrients. Soy flour provides additional calcium. If you don't mind the added fat, chopped pecans or hazelnuts can be stirred into most biscuit doughs. Sprinkle tops with sugar and cinnamon and bake. These biscuits are sure to please.

My all time favorite biscuits are *Fluffy Refrigerator Biscuits*. This bread is perfect for Sunday brunch since the dough is easily made ahead of time. Simply store batter, covered, in the refrigerator. When ready to use, spoon onto prepared pans and bake. The result is a fluffy, tender biscuit, as fine as the best Sunday dinner rolls.

CRANBERRY SCONES WITH ORANGE FROSTING

Golden scones are a great accompaniment to a summer buffet.

SCONES
1 1/2 cups unbleached all-purpose flour
3 tablespoons soy flour
2 1/2 teaspoons baking powder
3/4 teaspoon salt
3 tablespoons cooking oil
1/2 cup buttermilk, low fat
1/2 cup tofu, drained and mashed
1/2 cup dried cranberries, chopped

ORANGE FROSTING
2 to 3 teaspoons orange juice
2 cups confectioners sugar

Preheat oven to 425°F.

Combine all-purpose flour, soy flour, baking powder, and salt. In a food processor or blender, mix oil, buttermilk, and tofu. Stir wet ingredients into dry, blending just until mixed. Add cranberries. Knead dough with your hands until it's pliable and easy to handle.

Form dough into a ball. Turn onto a lightly floured surface. Shape to 7-inch circle. Using a sharp knife dusted with flour, cut dough into 12 wedges. Coat large baking sheet with nonstick cooking spray. Arrange 1/2 inch apart. Brush tops lightly with regular milk.

Bake 16 to 18 minutes or until lightly browned. Transfer to a serving plate.

While scones are baking, stir orange juice into confectioners sugar, adding more liquid, if necessary. Mixture should be thin. Drizzle over baked scones. Serve hot.

Yield: 12 scones

Nutrition Per Serving
Calories: 179
Total fat: 3.8 g
Cholesterol: 0
Carbohydrates: 33 g
Dietary fiber: 0.7 g
Protein: 4 g

Health Benefit: Per 1 cup serving, cranberries have 620 IU of vitamin A, 10 mg of vitamin C, and 18 mg of calcium.

FROSTED RAISIN CINNAMON SCONES

Not only are these scones chocked-full of raisins and spice, they also make a lovely presentation with a minimum of effort.

SCONES
1 1/2 cups unbleached all-purpose flour
3 tablespoons soy flour
2 1/2 teaspoons baking powder
3/4 teaspoon salt
1/2 teaspoon cinnamon
3 tablespoons cooking oil
1/2 cup low-fat buttermilk
1/2 cup tofu, drained and mashed
1/2 cup chopped raisins

FROSTING
2 to 4 teaspoons water
2 cups confectioners sugar

Preheat oven to 425°F.

Combine all-purpose flour, soy flour, baking powder, salt, and cinnamon.

In food processor or blender, mix oil, buttermilk, and tofu. Stir wet ingredients into dry. Blend just until mixed. Add raisins. Knead dough with hands until pliable and easy to handle.

Form dough into a ball. Turn onto lightly floured surface. Shape to 7-inch circle. Using a sharp knife dusted with flour, cut dough into 12 wedges. Coat large baking sheet with nonstick cooking spray. Arrange 1/2-inch apart. Brush tops lightly with milk.

Bake 16 to 18 minutes, or until lightly browned. Transfer to a serving plate.

While scones are baking, stir water into confectioners sugar. Mixture should be thin. Drizzle over baked scones. Serve hot.

Yield: 12 scones

Nutrition Per Serving
Calories: 197
Total fat: 3.9 g
Cholesterol: 0
Carbohydrates: 38 g
Dietary fiber: 1 g
Protein: 4 g

Health Benefit: Raisins are nutritious, fiber-rich fruits. A one-cup serving contains 5.8 g of dietary fiber and a whopping 1,089 mg of potassium, plus 71 mg of calcium, 3.0 mg of iron, and 0.4 mg of zinc as well as small amounts of vitamin A and the B vitamins.

APRICOT AND DATE SCONES

Apricots are just one of the many luscious fruits you can pack into scones.

1 1/2 cups unbleached all-purpose flour
3 tablespoons soy flour
2 1/2 teaspoons baking powder
3/4 teaspoon salt
3 tablespoons cooking oil
1/2 cup low-fat buttermilk
1/2 cup tofu, drained and mashed
1/2 teaspoon lemon extract
1/4 cup chopped dates
1/4 cup chopped dried apricots

ORANGE FROSTING
2 to 3 teaspoons orange juice
2 cups confectioners sugar

Preheat oven to 425°F.

Combine all-purpose flour, soy flour, baking powder, and salt.

In food processor or blender, mix oil, buttermilk, tofu, and lemon extract. Stir wet ingredients into dry. Blend just until mixed. Add dates and apricots. Knead dough until pliable and easy to handle.

Form dough into a ball. Turn onto lightly floured surface. Shape to 7-inch circle. Using a sharp knife dusted with flour, cut dough into 12 wedges. Coat a large baking sheet with nonstick cooking spray. Arrange 1/2-inch apart. Brush tops lightly with milk.

Bake 16 to 18 minutes or until lightly browned. Transfer to a serving plate.

While scones are baking, stir orange juice into confectioners sugar, adding more liquid, if necessary. Mixture should be thin. Drizzle over baked scones. Serve hot.

Yield: 12 scones

Nutrition Per Serving
Calories: 195
Total fat: 3.8 g
Cholesterol: 0
Carbohydrates: 37.4 g
Dietary fiber: 1.3 g
Protein: 3.6 g

Health Benefit: Apricots are packed with vitamin A, with a 1/4-cup serving containing 858 mg. Apricots contain some fiber and potassium, as well as 5 mg of calcium.

GARLIC AND CHEESE SCONES

Full of rich Italian flavor, these scones are perfect with salad and lasagna.

1 1/2 cups unbleached all-purpose flour
3 tablespoons soy flour
2 1/2 teaspoons baking powder
3/4 teaspoon salt
1/2 teaspoon parsley
1/4 teaspoon basil
1 large clove garlic, minced
1 1/2 cups grated fat-free mozzarella cheese
3 tablespoons cooking oil
1/2 cup low-fat buttermilk
1/2 cup tofu, drained and mashed

Preheat oven to 425°F.

Combine unbleached flour, soy flour, baking powder, and salt. Stir in parsley, basil, garlic, and 1 cup cheese.

In a food processor or blender, mix oil, buttermilk, and tofu. Stir wet ingredients into dry. Blend just until mixed. Knead dough until pliable and easy to handle.

Form dough into a ball. Turn onto a lightly floured surface. Shape to 7-inch circle. Using a sharp knife dusted with flour, cut dough into 12 wedges. Coat a large baking sheet with nonstick cooking spray. Arrange1/2-inch apart. Sprinkle remaining cheese over tops.

Bake 16 to 18 minutes or until lightly browned. Transfer to a serving plate. Serve warm.

Yield: 12 servings

Nutrition Per Serving
Calories: 124
Total fat: 3.8 g
Cholesterol: 3
Carbohydrates: 15 g
Dietary fiber: 0.7 g
Protein: 7 g

Health Benefit: One clove of garlic contains 5 mg of calcium, a small amount of potassium, a trace of dietary fiber, and 2 tablespoons of basil contains 5 mg of calcium, 131 IU of vitamin A, and 2.2 mcg of folacin.

SOY BISCUITS

Full of soy's goodness, these biscuits are heart-healthy and delicious.

2 cups prepackaged buttermilk biscuit/baking mix
1/2 cup soy flour
2 cups low-fat buttermilk

Preheat oven to 400°F.

Combine biscuit mix, soy flour, and buttermilk, stirring until ingredients are moistened. Shape dough to form 2 to 3 inch biscuits. Coat 2 baking sheets with nonstick cooking spray. Arrange biscuits 1/2 inch apart.

Bake 18 to 20 minutes or until golden brown.

Yield: 18 biscuits

Nutrition Per Serving
Calories: 77
Total fat: 2.4 g
Cholesterol: 1 mg
Carbohydrates: 10.8 g
Dietary fiber: 0.8 g
Protein: 3.3 g

Health Benefit: For each one-cup serving, soy flour contains an amazing 2,113 mg of potassium as well as 173 mg of calcium, 5.4 mg of iron, 3 mg of zinc, and 101 IU of vitamin A.

FLUFFY REFRIGERATOR BISCUITS

More like dinner rolls than biscuits, these easy, quick rolls will be a big family favorite in your home.

1 package active dry yeast
1/2 cup warm water (110°F to 115°F)
2 1/4 cups unbleached all-purpose flour
1/4 cup soy flour, sifted
1/2 teaspoon baking soda
1 teaspoon baking powder
1 teaspoon salt
2 tablespoons granulated sugar
1/4 cup olive oil
1 cup buttermilk

Dissolve yeast in warm water. Set aside. Combine all-purpose flour, soy flour, baking soda, baking powder, salt, and sugar. Stir in oil and buttermilk. Pour in yeast mixture. Stir until well blended. Cover. Refrigerate until ready to use. Preheat oven to 400° F.

Punch down. Knead on floured surface, working in enough all-purpose flour to make a soft dough that can be rolled. Roll to 1/4-inch thickness. Using a biscuit cutter, cut dough circles. Coat baking sheets with nonstick cooking spray. Arrange circles 1/2 inch apart. Allow to rise slightly. Bake 12 to 15 minutes or until golden brown. Yield: 30 biscuits

Nutrition Per Serving
Calories: 61
Total fat: 2 g
Cholesterol: 0 mg
Carbohydrates: 8.9 g
Dietary fiber: 0.4 g
Protein: 1.8

Health Benefit: Per one cup serving, soy flour has 39 mg of vitamin B6, 0.49 mg vitamin B1, and 0.97 mg of vitamin B2.

SWEET POTATO BISCUITS

Because sweet potatoes are so wonderfully healthy, we wanted to include them in one of our biscuit recipes. These delectable biscuits are perfect with ham, chicken, or roast beef.

2 cups buttermilk biscuit mix
3/4 cup nonfat milk
1/4 cup soy flour
3/4 cup sweet potato, baked, peeled, and mashed
2 tablespoons granulated sugar
1/4 cup cooking oil

Preheat oven to 400°F.

Combine biscuit mix, milk, soy flour, sweet potato, sugar, and cooking oil, stirring until ingredients are moistened.

Shape dough to form 3-inch biscuits. Coat large baking sheet with nonstick cooking spray. Arrange biscuits 1/2-inch apart. Bake 18 to 20 minutes or until golden brown.

Yield: 15 biscuits

Nutrition Per Serving
Calories: 117
Total fat: 5.8 g
Cholesterol: 0
Carbohydrates: 14 g
Dietary Fiber 0.2 g
Protein: 2.4 g

Health Benefit: Sweet potatoes are rich in beta-carotene and fiber.

Old Time Favorite Corn Bread

CORN BREAD

Corn bread and corn muffins are some of my favorites, so naturally I wanted to include those recipes in this cookbook. To make corn bread more than just delicious, use whole-grain cornmeal, which contains more fiber, lysine, and other important nutrients. Once you try whole-grain cornmeal, you'll never make corn bread any other way.

When using whole-grain cornmeal, be sure to use recipes which call for whole-grain cornmeal. In some recipes a one-on-one substitution of regular cornmeal for whole-grain may be fine, but in others the amount of liquid may need to be adjusted.

Recipes in this section include corn bread made with tomatoes and green chilies, a delightfully delicious way to serve corn bread. Full of buttermillk, corn kernels, and soy flour, this bread is almost healthy enough to be a meal in itself. Mexican Corn Muffins are another taste treat that are nutritous as well. These muffins rise high and are coarse textured.

The Soy Corn Bread included here is not only a healthy and easy way to serve corn bread for any meal, this lower fat version can readily be enjoyed by those on cholesterol restricted diets or those simply needing to reduce fat. So, even if you have special dietary needs or simply want to eat healthier food, you can easily treat your family, as well as your guests, to crusty and nourishing corn bread. Serving your own bread is always a rewarding experience.

Note: Use only low-fat silken tofu.

TOMATO AND GREEN CHILI CORN BREAD

Full of real south-of-the-boarder flavor, these muffins make a good accompaniment to hearty, vegetable soup, stew, potato soup, or chili.

3/4 cup unbleached all-purpose flour
1/4 cup soy flour
1 1/4 cups whole-grain cornmeal
3 teaspoons baking powder
1 teaspoon salt
1/2 teaspoon baking soda
1/4 teaspoon chili powder
2 egg whites
1/2 cup tomatoes and green chilies, diced and drained
1/4 cup granulated sugar
1 cup low-fat buttermilk
1 cup small frozen corn kernels
1/4 cup cooking oil
2 tablespoons baby food prunes

Preheat oven to 400°F. Combine all-purpose flour, soy flour, cornmeal, baking powder, salt, baking soda, and chili powder. Stir in egg whites, tomatoes and chilies, sugar, buttermilk, corn, oil, and prunes, mixing just until moistened. Do not overmix.

Coat 9 x 13 inch baking pan with nonstick cooking spray. Spoon in the batter. Bake 13 to 15 minutes. Serve hot.

Yield: 12 servings

Nutrition Per Serving
Calories: 164
Total fat: 5.5 g
Cholesterol: 1 mg
Carbohydrates: 25 g
Dietary fiber: 3 g
Protein: 5 g

Health Benefit: Tomatoes are an excellent source of vitamin A, with a half-cup serving containing close to 800 IU.

MEXICAN CORN MUFFINS

At the test kitchen, we love corn bread in any form. These unique spicy corn muffins rise high and are tender, moist, and delicious.

1 3/4 cup unbleached all-purpose flour
1/4 cup soy flour
3/4 cup whole-grain cornmeal
1/4 cup granulated sugar
3/4 teaspoon baking soda
3/4 teaspoon salt
2 egg whites
1 1/4 cups buttermilk
3 tablespoons cooking oil
3/4 cup frozen corn
1 small jalapeño pepper
2 tablespoons dried onion

Preheat oven to 350°F.

In large bowl, combine all-purpose flour, soy flour, cornmeal, sugar, baking soda, and salt. Remove seeds from pepper. Finely chop pepper. Stir in egg whites, buttermilk, oil, corn, jalapeño pepper, and dried onion. Mix just enough to moisten dry ingredients.

Coat muffin tin with nonstick cooking spray. Spoon in batter, filling the cups two-thirds full. Bake 20 to 25 minutes or until a toothpick inserted in center comes out clean.

Yield: 12 muffins

Nutrition Per Serving
Calories: 176
Total fat: 4.1
Cholesterol: 1 mg
Carbohydrates: 29 g
Dietary fiber: 1.6 g
Protein: 5 g

Health Benefit: Per one-cup serving, soy flour contains 3.6 mg of niacin.

SOY CORN BREAD FROM A MIX

Since this delicious soy-boosted version is made from a mix, it can be whipped out anytime.

2 cups self-rising cornmeal mix
3 tablespoons granulated sugar
1 1/4 cups low-fat soy milk
1/4 cup tofu, drained and mashed
1 egg white
1 tablespoon plus 1 teaspoon cooking oil
1 tablespoon plus 1 teaspoon baby food prunes

Preheat oven to 425°F.

Combine cornmeal mix, sugar, soy milk, tofu, egg white, oil, and baby food prunes.

Coat a 10-inch skillet with nonstick cooking spray. Pour batter into skillet. Bake 20 to 25 minutes or until a toothpick inserted in the center comes out clean.

Yield: 8 to 10 servings

Nutrition Per Serving
Calories: 165
Total fat: 3.3
Cholesterol: 0
Carbohydrates: 31 g
Dietary fiber: 1 g
Protein: 4 g

Health Benefit: Soy flour is rich in folacin, having 289 mcg per one cup serving.

Notes

Healthy Pancakes and Waffles

PANCAKES AND WAFFLES

Kids of all ages love pancakes and waffles, so why not boost them nutritionally and serve them more often? Fortified with fiber, protein, and dozens of other nutrients, these pancakes and waffles are good for breakfast, lunch, or dinner. Some recipes were created with prepackaged mixes to show how easy it is to add soy products, like tofu and soy flour, to almost any recipe. A variety of whole-grain products—such as defatted soy flour, whole-wheat flour, and flaxseed meal— were incorporated to increase the nutritive value of this outstanding anytime food.

For both pancakes and waffles, I personally like to use low-fat soy milk in place of nonfat dairy milk.

Be creative when serving pancakes and waffles. Top them with nonfat dessert topping, apples, maple syrup, light peach butter, blackberries, raspberries, or any combination of fruit. Be creative with syrups, as well. Mix grated lemon or orange peel with maple syrup and spoon on top for a simple, yet delicious, alternative.

Although we do not bake pancakes and waffles in the oven, we do bake them, in a sense, on griddles, so I wanted to include these delicious, healthy recipes for you to try.

Tip: *When working with tofu, be sure to drain and mash it well before adding to recipes.* **Use only low-fat silken tofu.**

PLUM SPICE BELGIAN WAFFLES

A mix makes these spicy waffles easy.

1 1/4 cups Belgian waffle mix
3/4 cup plus 2 tablespoons nonfat milk
1/4 cup soy flour
1/4 cup brown sugar, packed
1 jar baby food strained plums, 2 1/2 ounces
2 egg whites
1 tablespoon cooking oil
1/2 teaspoon allspice
1/2 teaspoon ginger
1/2 teaspoon cinnamon
1/4 cup chopped walnuts, toasted (optional)
1/2 cup raisins

In large bowl, combine waffle mix, milk, soy flour, sugar, plums, egg whites, oil, allspice, ginger, and cinnamon. Stir just enough to moisten ingredients. Do not overmix. Gently fold in walnuts and raisins. Batter will be lumpy.

Coat waffle iron with nonstick cooking spray and heat. Spoon on approximately 1/2 cup batter for each waffle. Cook 3 to 4 minutes until golden brown or according to waffle iron directions.

Yield: 6 to 7 large waffles

Nutrition Per Serving
Calories: 200
Total fat: 2.8
Cholesterol: 1 mg
Carbohydrates: 38.7 g
Dietary fiber: 1.7 g
Protein: 6.6 g

Health Benefit: Plums are rich in potassium, containing 473 mg per one-cup serving.

BLUEBERRY AMARANTH
BELGIAN WAFFLES

Amaranth adds nutrients and flavor to these delicious blueberry waffles.

1 1/3 cups Belgian waffle mix
1/4 cup soy flour
1/4 cup amaranth flour
1/2 cup egg substitute (or 2 egg whites)
1 tablespoon cooking oil
1 cup applesauce
1/2 cup nonfat milk
1/2 cup blueberries

In medium bowl, combine waffle mix, soy flour, amaranth flour, egg substitute, cooking oil, applesauce, and milk. Stir just enough to moisten ingredients. Do not overmix. Add blueberries, stirring gently. Batter will be lumpy.

Coat waffle iron with nonstick cooking spray and heat. Spoon on approximately 1/2 cup batter for each waffle. Cook 3 or 4 minutes until golden brown or according to waffle iron directions.

Yield: 8 large waffles

Nutrition Per Serving
Calories: 167
Total fat: 2.7
Cholesterol: 0 mg
Carbohydrates: 30.6 g
Dietary fiber: 2.1 g
Protein: 5.9 g

Health Benefit: Blueberries contain 126 mg of potassium, 142 IU vitamin A, plus a small amount of fiber, iron, and zinc.

SOY BELGIAN WAFFLES

These are the good old-fashioned kind of waffles--tender and sweet.

1 1/4 cups Belgian waffle mix
1/4 cup soy flour
1 1/2 teaspoons Ener-G™ egg substitute mixed
  with 2 tablespoons water
1 tablespoon cooking oil
1 1/2 cups plus 2 tablespoons nonfat milk or soy milk
1/2 cup applesauce

In medium bowl, combine waffle mix, soy flour, egg substitute, oil, milk, and applesauce.

Coat waffle iron with nonstick cooking spray and heat. Spoon on approximatley 1/2 cup of batter for each waffle. Cook 3 to 4 minutes until golden brown or according to waffle iron directions.

Yield: 5 to 6 waffles

Nutrition Per Serving
Calories: 190
Total fat: 3.3 g
Cholesterol: 1 mg
Carbohydrates: 32.4 g
Dietary fiber: 1.8 g
Protein: 8.5 g

Health Benefit: One cup of soy flour has 8 g of dietary fiber.

RAISIN CINNAMON WAFFLES

Serve these spicy and delicious waffles with warm maple syrup as a guaranteed crowd pleaser.

1 egg white, slightly beaten
1 cup nonfat milk
1 tablespoon granulated sugar
1 1/4 cups low-fat buttermilk pancake mix
1 tablespoon cooking oil
1/4 cup soy flour
1/4 teaspoon cinnamon
1/2 cup raisins

In medium bowl, combine egg white, milk, sugar, pancake mix, oil, soy flour, cinnamon, and raisins. Mix until well blended.

Coat waffle iron with nonstick cooking spray and heat. Spoon on approximately 1/2 cup batter for each waffle. Cook 3 to 4 minutes until golden brown or follow the waffle iron directions.

Yield: 5 to 6 waffles

Nutrition Per Serving
Calories: 220
Total fat: 2.9 g
Cholesterol: 1 mg
Carbohydrates: 49 g
Dietary fiber: 2 g
Protein: 7 g

Health Benefit: Raisins are a healthful treat, with one cup containing 1,089 mg of potassium, 4.8 mcg of folacin, 1.2 mg of niacin, and 3.0 mg iron. If counting calories, raisins contain 435 calories per cup.

SOUTHERN CORNMEAL PANCAKES

Cornmeal provides an intriguing texture to these pancakes. Top with honey, syrup, or blueberries.

1 1/4 cups unbleached all-purpose flour
2 tablespoons soy flour
3/4 cup whole-grain cornmeal
2 tablespoons granulated sugar
1 1/2 teaspoons baking powder
1 1/2 teaspoons baking soda
1/4 teaspoon salt
3 egg whites, slightly beaten
1 1/2 cups low-fat buttermilk
1/4 cup cooking oil

Combine unbleached flour, soy flour, cornmeal, sugar, baking powder, baking soda, and salt. Stir in egg whites, buttermilk, and cooking oil, mixing just until ingredients are blended. Batter may be lumpy.

Coat griddle or pan with nonstick cooking spray. Spoon batter in large dollops. Cook 1 or 2 minutes on each side, flipping pancakes when bubbles on edges begin to break and turn dry. Serve warm with maple syrup, honey, or your favorite fruit.

Yield: 12 medium pancakes

Nutrition Per Serving
Calories: 134
Total fat: 5.3 g
Cholesterol: 1 mg
Carbohydrates: 18 g
Dietary fiber: 1 g
Protein: 4 g

Health Benefit: Whole-grain cornmeal is fiber rich, with a 1 cup serving containing 18.3 g. It has 350 mg of potassium, 4.2 mg of iron, and 2.2 mg of zinc.

QUICK AND EASY HEART HEALTHY SOY PANCAKES

I gave this recipe to my mother, and she loved it. After a few weeks, all of her friends were making these healthier pancakes. Soy-enriched foods are perfect for us as we age because soy has the extra vitamins, minerals, and protein that aging bodies need. Treat your Mom to these.

1/2 cup tofu, drained and mashed
1 2/3 cups nonfat milk
2 tablespoons soy flour
2 cups nonfat buttermilk pancake mix
1/4 cup wheat germ

In medium mixing bowl, beat tofu, milk, and soy flour. By hand, stir in pancake mix and wheat germ, mixing just enough to moisten ingredients. Do not overmix. Batter will be lumpy. Coat griddle with nonstick cooking spray and heat. Spoon batter in large dollops. Cook 1 to 2 minutes on each side, flipping pancakes when bubbles on the edges begin to break and turn dry.

Yield: 10 servings

Nutrition Per Serving
Calories: 113
Total fat: 0.6 g
Cholesterol: 1 mg
Carbohydrates: 22.3 g
Dietary fiber: 0.4 g
Protein: 5.5 g

Health Benefit: Many studies conclude that foods containing protein from soybeans, as part of a diet low in saturated fat and cholesterol, may reduce the risk of heart disease by lowering the blood's LDL cholesterol.

ENERGY-RICH BLUEBERRY PANCAKES

Full of complex grains and sweet blueberries, these pancakes are nutritious and delicious—the perfect combination for morning or evening meals.

1/2 cup tofu, drained and mashed
2 cups nonfat milk
1/2 cup unbleached all-purpose flour
2 cups nonfat or low fat buttermilk pancake mix
1/2 cup fresh blueberries, washed and drained

In medium bowl, beat tofu, milk, and flour. Batter will be lumpy. By hand, add pancake mix, stirring just enough to moisten the ingredients. Do not overmix. Gently stir in blueberries. If batter is thick, thin with a bit of milk.

Coat griddle with nonstick cooking spray and heat. Spoon batter in large dollops. Cook 1 to 2 minutes on each side, flipping pancakes when bubbles on edges begin to break and turn dry.

Yield: 10 servings

Nutrition Per Serving (per low-fat pancake mix)
Calories: 128.6
Total fat: 0.4 g
Cholesterol: 1 mg
Carbohydrates: 26.5 g
Dietary fiber: 0.4 g
Protein: 5.2 g

Health Benefit: Tofu adds possible cancer-fighting properties and could aid in lowering bad cholesterol.

Variation: *Substitute up to 2 tablespoons soy flour for 2 tablespoons all-purpose flour.*

AMARANTH PANCAKES

Here at the test kitchen, we like to include amaranth flour in baked goods. Amaranth flour easily adds nutrition, and its nutty flavor is delicious.

1 cup plus 2 tablespoons nonfat buttermilk pancake mix
1 cup nonfat milk
1/4 cup amaranth flour
2 tablespoons soy flour
1 tablespoon olive oil
2 egg whites, slightly beaten

In medium mixing bowl, combine pancake mix, milk, amaranth flour, soy flour, oil, and egg whites. Stir just enough to moisten ingredients. Do not overmix. Batter will be lumpy.

Coat griddle with nonstick cooking spray and heat. Spoon batter in large dollops. Cook 1 to 2 minutes on each side, flipping pancakes when bubbles on edges begin to break and turn dry.

Yield: 6 pancakes

Nutrition Per Serving
Calories: 104
Total fat: 2 g
Cholesterol: 1 mg
Carbohydrates: 18 g
Dietary fiber: 0.5 g
Protein: 4 g

Health Benefit: Amaranth flour is high in fiber and quality protein. A quarter-cup serving contains only 1.5 g of fat, no saturated fat or sodium, and 110 mg of potassium.

Pizza, Flatbread, and Focaccia

PIZZA, FLATBREAD, AND FOCACCIA

Pizza. The very word evokes juicy, plump tomatoes, sweet-smelling basil, pungently rich oregano, mozzarella and Parmesan cheese, all dashed with a splash of olive oil. This delicious dish is one of America's best loved foods and with good reason. Teens and kids especially love pizza, and now you can make favorite dishes healthier, with less fat and more nutrition.

Whether you choose Deep Dish Pizza, Sun-Dried Tomato Pizza, or Spinach Cheese Stuffed Pizza, these recipes offer healthy goodness in every bite. Today's pizza has more than a new look. Underneath, crusts are made with whole wheat or cornmeal, and all the recipes included here are laced with healthful soy.

Besides enriching the pizza dough with whole grains, bits of garlic, herbs, cheese, or pesto add a delightful aroma as a soft or crisp, thin or thick, pizza bakes and turns the color of golden wheat.

PIZZA TIPS

When adding tofu to pizza dough, use a food processor or blender to process the tofu. Tofu blends well when creamed with sugar, butter, or oil, but it doesn't mix well with water or milk without the benefit of processing or blending.

Buy the best canned tomatoes you can afford. Some brands are watery. I prefer to use the crushed variety when making pizza sauce.

SPINACH CHEESE STUFFED PIZZA

Made with spinach and cheese, this pizza is a perfect vegetarian meal.

PIZZA DOUGH
2 teaspoons sugar
2 packages active dry yeast
1 1/2 cups warm water (110°F to 115°F)
3 cups unbleached all-purpose flour
1/4 cup vital gluten
3 teaspoons salt
1/4 cup olive oil
2 tablespoons nonfat milk
3 tablespoons soy flour, sifted

SAUCE
1 can (16 ounces) crushed tomatoes, drained
1 tablespoon olive oil
3/4 teaspoon dried oregano
1 teaspoon dried basil
1/4 teaspoon salt
1 garlic clove, finely minced
2 tablespoons fat-free Parmesan cheese

FILLING
1 package (10 ounces) frozen chopped spinach, thawed
1 package (8 ounces) fat-free grated mozzarella cheese

TO MAKE DOUGH
Using food processor, combine sugar, yeast, and warm water, processing until yeast dissolves. Stop machine. Add 2 cups all-purpose flour, vital gluten, salt, oil, and milk. Process 1 to 2 minutes. Turn off machine. (Can use mixer.) Add remaining all-purpose flour and soy flour. Mix with a start-and-stop action until thoroughly combined. Mixture will be thick, so don't leave machine constantly running. Turn dough onto a lightly floured surface. Knead gently until soft and pliable.

Place dough in bowl coated with nonstick cooking spray, turning once to oil top. Cover and let rise in warm place until doubled, about 2 to 3 hours.

Punch dough down, and turn onto a floured work surface. Knead 1 to 2 minutes, adding the slightest amount of flour. Divide dough in two pieces, one slightly larger. Roll larger piece to a 15-inch circle. Coat pizza pan with nonstick cooking spray. Place dough on pan, pushing into bottom and sides. Trim off excess. Roll second portion to 12-inch circle and set aside.

TO MAKE SAUCE
In small bowl, combine sauce ingredients. Do not cook.

TO MAKE FILLING AND ASSEMBLE PIZZA
Preheat oven to 425°F. Using a food processor or mixer, process spinach 30 seconds. Pour into a bowl; add mozzarella cheese and stir.

Spread half the sauce over crust. Top with spinach mixture. Cover with smaller crust. Pinch two layers of dough together. Spread remaining sauce on top. Cut slits in crust to allow steam to escape. Top with additional mozzarella cheese, if desired, and brush the edges with olive oil. Bake on lowest oven rack 10 minutes. Move to middle rack. Bake an additional 25 to 30 minutes or until crust is lightly browned.

Yield: 10 servings

Nutrition Per Serving
Calories: 248
Total fat: 7 g
Cholesterol 1 mg
Carbohydrates: 35 g
Dietary fiber: 3.5 g
Protein: 10.2 g

Health Benefit: Spinach is part of a healthy diet because it contains vitamin A, iron, calcium, and B vitamins such as folacin.

EGGPLANT PARMESAN
CHEESE CALZONE

Eggplant and cheese combine here to make a winning, meat-free dish.

DOUGH
1 teaspoon sugar
1 package active dry yeast
1 cup warm water (110°F to 115°F)
1/2 cup nonfat milk
2 tablespoons olive oil
1 teaspoon salt
3 cups unbleached all-purpose flour
1/4 cup vital gluten
1/2 cup whole-grain cornmeal
2 tablespoons soy flour, sifted

FILLING
1 tablespoon olive oil
1 medium finely chopped eggplant
2 tablespoons chopped parsley
1/4 teaspoon pepper
1/4 teaspoon dried oregano
1/2 cup finely chopped onion
1/2 cup chopped mushrooms
1/4 cup nonfat grated mozzarella cheese
1/4 cup nonfat grated Parmesan cheese

SAUCE
1 can (16 ounces) crushed tomatoes, drained
1 tablespoon olive oil
3/4 teaspoon dried oregano
1 teaspoon dried basil
1/2 teaspoon salt
1 clove garlic, finely chopped

TO MAKE PIZZA DOUGH

Using a food processor or a mixer, combine sugar, yeast, and warm water, processing until yeast dissolves. Stop machine. Add milk, oil, salt, 2 cups all-purpose flour, and vital gluten. Process 1 to 2 minutes. Turn off machine. Add remaining all-purpose flour, cornmeal, and soy flour. Mix with a start-and-stop action until thoroughly combined. If too thick, stir by hand.

Turn dough onto lightly floured surface. Knead until soft and pliable. Place in a bowl coated with nonstick cooking spray, turning once. Cover and let rise in warm place until doubled, about 2 to 3 hours. Punch down. Turn onto floured work surface. Knead 1 to 2 minutes, adding the slightest amount of flour. Divide into 10 equal sections. On lightly floured surface, roll each section to 1/8 inch thick circle that is 6 inch diameter. Brush surface with olive oil, if desired.

TO MAKE FILLING AND ASSEMBLE

Coat skillet with olive oil. Peel and finely chop eggplant. Add eggplant and parsley; sauté until eggplant softens. Stir in pepper, oregano, onion, and mushrooms. Remove from heat; add mozzarella and Parmesan cheese. Place small amount of eggplant mixture in center of each circle. Moisten edges with beaten egg white. Fold to half circle, pressing edges firmly together. If desired, brush outside of calzone lightly with olive oil. Coat large baking sheet with nonstick cooking spray. Place calzones on pan. Cover with towel and let rise, about 1 hour.

Preheat oven to 375°F. Bake calzones 20 to 28 minutes or until golden brown. Remove to a serving platter. Combine sauce ingredients, stirring to blend. Heat before serving. Pour over calzones. Yield: 10 large servings

Nutrition Per Serving
Calories: 263
Total fat: 6 g
Cholesterol: 0
Carbohydrates: 42 g
Dietary fiber: 4 g
Protein: 10 g

Health Benefit: Eggplant contains folacin and traces of other B vitamins.

DEEP-DISH PIZZA

Thick, tender crust full of spicy sauce—this pizza is a winner any day of the week and any week of the year.

PIZZA DOUGH
2 packages active dry yeast
3/4 cup warm water (110°F to 115°F)
1/2 cup nonfat milk
1 teaspoon salt
1/4 cup olive oil
2 1/2 cups unbleached all-purpose flour
1/4 cup vital gluten
3 tablespoons soy flour, sifted

SAUCE AND TOPPING
1 can (28 ounces) crushed tomatoes, drained
1 tablespoon olive oil
3/4 teaspoon dried oregano
1 teaspoon dried basil
1/4 to 1/2 teaspoon salt, to taste
1 garlic clove, finely minced
1/2 cup fat-free grated mozzarella cheese
2 cups ricotta cheese

TO MAKE DOUGH
Using food processor, combine yeast and warm water, processing until yeast dissolves. Stop machine. Add milk, salt, oil, 2 cups all-purpose flour, and vital gluten.

Process 1 to 2 minutes. Turn off machine. Add remaining all-purpose flour and soy flour. Mix with a start-and-stop action until thoroughly combined. Mixture will be thick, so don't leave machine constantly running. (Can use mixer.)

Turn dough onto lightly floured surface. Knead gently until dough is soft and pliable.

Place dough in bowl coated with nonstick cooking spray, turning once to oil top. Cover and let rise in warm place until doubled, about 2 to 3 hours. (If desired, cover dough with plastic wrap and refrigerate overnight. When ready to use, bring dough to room temperature. Proceed with recipe.)

Punch dough down. Turn onto floured work surface. Knead 1 to 2 minutes, adding the slightest amount of flour. Divide dough in half. Roll each piece to a 10-inch circle.

Coat two 10-inch pizza pans with nonstick cooking spray. Place one circle of dough into each pan, pushing into bottom and sides. Roll up sides of dough to form a thick edge. Cover each pan. Let rise in a warm place, about 30 minutes.

TO MAKE SAUCE AND ASSEMBLE PIZZAS
Preheat oven to 425°F.

In small bowl, combine tomatoes, oil, oregano, basil, salt, and garlic cloves. Stir to blend. Do not cook.

Spread half of the mozzarella and half of the ricotta cheese over each crust. Pour half of the sauce over each. Bake 20 to 25 minutes.

Yield: two 10-inch pizzas (8 servings each)

Nutrition Per Serving
Calories: 190
Total fat: 8.5 g
Cholesterol: 16 mg
Carbohydrates: 19 g
Dietary fiber: 1 g
Protein: 9 g

Health Benefit: Tomatoes are a good source of vitamin A, with a one-cup serving containing 1,245 IU of this important vitamin.

SUN-DRIED TOMATO WHOLE-WHEAT PIZZA

Spicy and tangy, this sun-dried tomato version is combined with herbs and whole-wheat for up-to-date nutrition.

MARINATED TOMATOES
6 ounces sun-dried tomatoes
6 tablespoons olive oil
3 to 4 cloves garlic, crushed

PIZZA DOUGH
1 teaspoon sugar
1 package active dry yeast
1 1/4 cups warm water (110°F to 115°F)
1/4 cup nonfat milk
3 tablespoons olive oil
1 teaspoon salt
2 1/2 cups unbleached all-purpose flour
1/4 cup vital gluten
1/2 cup fat-free Parmesan cheese
1/4 cup whole-wheat flour
2 tablespoons soy flour, sifted

CHEESE TOPPING
6 ounces fat-free grated mozzarella cheese
3/4 teaspoon dried basil
1/2 cup Parmesan cheese (optional)

TO MARINATE TOMATOES
Chop sun-dried tomatoes into bite-sized pieces. Put tomatoes, olive oil, and garlic in a container. Marinate at room temperature at least 1 hour.

TO MAKE DOUGH
Using a food processor or a mixer, combine sugar, yeast, and warm water, processing until yeast dissolves. Stop machine. Add milk, oil, salt, 2 cups all-purpose flour, and vital gluten.

Process 1-2 minutes. Turn off machine. Add remaining all-purpose flour, Parmesan cheese, whole-wheat flour, and soy flour. Mix with a start-and-stop action until thoroughly combined. Mixture will be thick, so don't leave machine constantly running.

Turn dough onto lightly floured surface. Knead gently until dough is soft and pliable. Place dough in bowl coated with nonstick cooking spray, turning once to oil top. Cover and let rise in warm place until doubled, about 2 to 3 hours.

Punch dough down. Turn onto work surface. Knead 1 to 2 minutes, adding the slightest amount of flour. Divide dough in half. Roll each piece to a 10-inch circle.

Coat two 10-inch pizza pans with nonstick cooking spray. Place one circle of dough into each pan, pushing into bottom and sides. Roll up sides of dough to form a thick edge. Cover each pan. Let dough rise in a warm place, about 30 minutes. Preheat oven to 450°F. Bake 5 to 6 minutes. Remove from oven.

TO ASSEMBLE PIZZAS
Evenly sprinkle mozzarella cheese on each prebaked crust. Spread sun-dried tomato marinade over each pizza. Pour on the oil. Sprinkle each pizza with dried basil. Add more Parmesan cheese, if desired. Bake at 450°F an additional 5 to 7 minutes, or until lightly brown.

Yield: 2 medium pizzas, 8 servings each

Nutrition Per Serving
Calories: 214
Total fat: 8 g
Cholesterol: 2 mg
Carbohydrates: 25 g
Dietary fiber: 2 g
Protein: 9 g

Health Benefit: Whole-wheat flour contains 14.6 g of dietary fiber and 486 mg of potassium per one-cup serving.

MUSHROOM-CHEESE PIZZA

Mushrooms, dripping with cheese, top a crisp crust that will please any pizza fan.

DOUGH
1 package active dry yeast
1 cup warm water (110°F to 115°F)
1 teaspoon sugar
1/2 teaspoon salt
1 tablespoon olive oil
2 cups unbleached all-purpose flour
1/4 cup soy flour, sifted

SAUCE
1 can (16 ounces) crushed tomatoes, drained
1 tablespoon olive oil
3/4 teaspoon dried oregano
1 teaspoon dried basil
1/2 teaspoon salt
1 garlic clove, finely chopped

TOPPING
1 cup sliced mushrooms
1/2 cup fat-free grated Parmesan cheese
1/4 cup fat-free grated mozzarella cheese

TO MAKE PIZZA DOUGH
Using food processor, combine yeast and warm water, processing until yeast dissolves. Stop machine. Add sugar, salt, oil, all-purpose flour, and soy flour. Process until smooth, using a start-and-stop action until thoroughly combined. (Can use mixer.)

Place dough in bowl coated with nonstick cooking spray, turning once to oil top. Cover and let rise in a warm place until doubled, about 1 hour. (If desired, cover dough with plastic wrap and refrigerate overnight. When ready to use, bring dough to room temperature and proceed with recipe.)

Punch dough down. Coat pizza stone or pan with nonstick cooking spray. Turn dough onto stone or pan. Spray hands with nonstick cooking spray. Stretch dough up to and over edges of stone or pan, rolling up sides of dough to form a thick edge. Cover and let rise in a warm place, about 30 minutes. Meanwhile, prepare sauce and topping.

TO MAKE SAUCE, TOPPING, AND ASSEMBLE PIZZA

Preheat oven to 425°F. In medium saucepan, combine sauce ingredients. Stir to blend. Heat sauce just before using.

Sauté mushrooms. When dough is ready, spoon on sauce; add mushrooms, Parmesan cheese, and mozzarella cheese. Bake 10 to 15 minutes or until crust is golden brown. Serve hot.

Yield: 8 servings

Nutrition Per Serving
Calories: 192
Total fat: 3.9 g
Cholesterol: 1 mg
Carbohydrates: 29 g
Dietary fiber: 2 g
Protein: 8 g

Health Benefit: One cup of mushrooms contains 251 mg of potassium, 14.3 mcg of folacin, and only 0.3 g of fat.

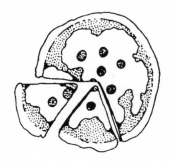

FLATBREAD

Topped with fruit, herbs, sugar, or spice, flatbread is versatile and s-o-o-o easy to make.

DOUGH
1 package active dry yeast
1 1/2 cups warm water (110°F to 115°F)
2 tablespoons olive oil
1 1/2 teaspoons salt
3 cups unbleached all-purpose flour
2 tablespoons soy flour, sifted
2 tablespoons powdered milk

Using food processor, combine yeast and water. With machine running, add oil and salt. Stop machine. Add 1 1/2 cups all-purpose flour. Process or beat 1 to 2 minutes. Add soy flour and powdered milk. Process or beat 1 to 2 minutes. Stop machine. Add remaining all-purpose flour. Process or beat using a start-and-stop action until well mixed. (Can use mixer.)

Turn dough onto lightly floured surface. Knead until smooth and pliable, about 3 to 5 minutes. Place dough in a bowl coated with nonstick cooking spray, turning once to oil the top. Cover and let rise in a warm place until doubled, about 1 to 3 hours. (If desired, cover dough with plastic wrap and refrigerate overnight. When ready to use, bring dough to room temperature and proceed with recipe.)

Punch dough down, and turn onto a lightly floured work surface. Knead 1 to 2 minutes, adding the slightest amount of flour. Divide dough into 3 pieces. Roll each piece into a ball. Cover and let rest 10 to 15 minutes. Coat three 9-inch pie pans with nonstick cooking spray. Spread each piece of dough into a pan, dimpling the dough with fingertips, leaving indentations throughout the dough as you spread it. Lightly brush tops with olive oil, using 1 tablespoon for all three rounds. Dimple dough as you work. Sprinkle lightly with salt to taste, if desired. If topping with fruit, omit salt.

Cover and let rise until doubled, about 1 hour. Add your favorite topping. Preheat oven to 425°F. Dimple dough again, and bake 15 to 18 minutes or until lightly golden. Cool slightly before serving.

TOPPING VARIATIONS:
Each recipe makes three 9-inch rounds.

Onion topping: Finely slice 2 onions. Sauté onions in 1 tablespoon olive oil. Sprinkle with 1 tablespoon dried basil.

Sweet pepper topping: Finely slice 2 yellow and red sweet peppers. Lightly sauté peppers in 1 tablespoon olive oil with a large minced garlic clove.

Eggplant topping: Use 1 or 2 whole eggplants, depending on size. Peel and slice very thinly. Soak slices in salted water at least 15 minutes. Drain and lightly sauté in 1 tablespoon olive oil with a large minced garlic clove. Drain on paper towel. Layer flatbread with thinly sliced medium-sized ripe tomatoes. Top with sautéed eggplant. Sprinkle with a thin layer of fat-free grated Parmesan cheese.

Blackberry topping: Use 1/4 cup blackberries sprinkled with 2 tablespoons turbinado sugar.

Blueberry-cream cheese topping: Use 1/4 cup blueberries and 1/4 cup fat-free cream cheese. Sprinkle with 2 tablespoons turbinado sugar.

Yield: 3 (9-inch) rounds, 6 servings each

Nutrition Per Serving
Calories: 111
Total fat: 2.8 g
Cholesterol: 1 mg
Carbohydrates: 18 g
Dietary fiber: 1 g
Protein: 3 g

Health Benefit: Onions are a good source of folacin, with one onion containing 30.4 mcg.

FOCACCIA

This healthier version of an Italian classic is equally delicious.

1 package active dry yeast
2 cups warm water (110°F to 115°F)
2 tablespoons olive oil
5 cups unbleached all-purpose flour
1/4 cup soy flour, sifted
1 tablespoon salt

HERB OLIVE OIL
1 tablespoon olive oil
1 tablespoon dried parsley
1 tablespoon dried basil
1 tablespoon chopped dried bay leaf
1 tablespoon dried minced onion

In medium mixing bowl, dissolve yeast in warm water. Stir in olive oil and 2 cups all-purpose flour. Beat 1 to 2 minutes. Stir in soy flour and salt, beating well, 1 to 2 minutes. Add remaining all-purpose flour.

Turn dough onto a lightly floured surface. Knead until soft and pliable, about 5 to 6 minutes. Place dough in a bowl coated with nonstick cooking spray, turning once to oil the top. Cover and let rise until doubled, about 1 to 2 hours. (If desired, cover dough with plastic wrap and refrigerate overnight. When ready to use, bring dough to room temperature and proceed with recipe.)

Punch dough down and knead 1-2 minutes. Divide into 2 pieces. Coat two 9 x 13-inch oblong pans with nonstick cooking spray. Shape each piece of dough to fit bottom of pan. Cover and let rise, about 30 minutes. Dimple dough with fingertips, leaving indentations about 1/2 inch throughout dough. Dimpling allows oils and herbs to catch in grooves, providing a rustic texture.

Make Herb Flavored Olive Oil by mixing ingredients in a small bowl. Brush oil on dough. Sprinkle lightly with salt. Cover and let dough rise in a warm place, about 1 to 2 hours.

Preheat oven to 375°F. Bake focaccia about 10 minutes or until tops are golden brown and just starting to bubble.

Yield: 24 slices

Nutrition Per Serving
Calories: 116
Total fat: 2 g
Cholesterol: 0
Carbohydrates: 21 g
Dietary fiber: 1 g
Protein: 3 g

Health Benefit: A tablespoon of parsley contains 303 IU of vitamin A, 10 mg of calcium, and 49 mg of potassium.

HERB-CHEESE FOCACCIA

Full of herbs, this bread is healthy and delicious.

1 package active dry yeast
2 cups warm water (110°F to 115°F)
3 tablespoons olive oil
5 cups unbleached all-purpose flour
1 teaspoon salt
1 teaspoon seasoned salt
1 teaspoon garlic powder
1 1/4 teaspoons dried Italian seasoning
1/4 cup soy flour, sifted
1/2 cup mozzarella cheese, fat free

In medium mixing bowl, dissolve yeast in warm water. Stir in 2 tablespoons of the olive oil, 2 cups all-purpose flour, salt, seasoned salt, garlic powder, and Italian seasoning. Beat 1 to 2 minutes. Stir in soy flour, beating well, 1 to 2 minutes. Add remaining all-purpose flour.

Turn dough onto a lightly floured surface. Knead until soft. Place in bowl coated with nonstick cooking spray, turning once. Cover. Let rise until doubled, 1 to 2 hours. Punch dough down. Knead 1 to 2 minutes. Divide into 2 pieces. Coat two 9 x 13-inch oblong pans with nonstick cooking spray. Shape dough to fit bottom of pans. Cover. Let rise, about 30 minutes. Dimple dough with fingertips. Brush remaining oil on top. Cover. Let rise, about 1 to 2 hours. Preneat oven to 375°F. Sprinkle dough with cheese. Bake 20 minute or until tops are golden brown. Yield: 24 servings.

Nutrition Per Serving
Calories: 121
Total fat: 2.4g
Cholesterol: 1 mg
Carbohydrates: 20.5 g
Dietary fiber: 0.9 g
Protein: 4 g

Health Benefit: Combined with cheese and soy flour, this bread is protein and calcium rich.

PIZZA CRUST FROM A MIX

Quick and easy from a mix. How simple can eating soy be?

1 package (6.5 ounces) pizza crust mix
1/2 cup plus 1 tablespoon hot water
2 tablespoons soy flour

Place oven rack in lowest position. Preheat oven to 450°F. Coat pizza pan with nonstick cooking spray.

Mix ingredients. Cover and let rest in a warm place 5 minutes. Using floured fingers, press dough into 12-inch circle on prepared pan. Top with favorite toppings.

Bake 12 to17 minutes or until crust is golden brown.

Yield: 8 servings

Nutrition Per Serving
Calories: 85
Total fat: 1 g
Cholesterol: 0 mg
Carbohydrates: 17 g
Dietary fiber: 0 g
Protein: 3 g

Health Benefit: Defatted soy flour contains vitamin-A , is low in fat, and is high in calcium and potassium.

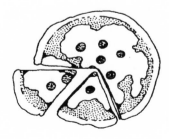

Notes

Glorious
Cakes

CAKES

Though it might seem a contradiction to have cake recipes in a cookbook devoted to healthy foods, the fact is modern-day cakes are frequently topped with fruits, such as strawberries, blueberries, and blackberries. And, of course, fruits contain a wide range of nutrients, including traces of zinc (essential for proper immune function), vitamin B6 (essential for metabolizing protein and fat), and vitamin C (essential for proper nerve functioning, normal bone growth, and blood sugar regulation). Containing antioxidant properties, as well as calcium and potassium, fruits are some of the healthiest foods on earth. These naturally healthy foods make for natural and healthy additions to cake. With soyfoods added, cakes are more nutritious and preserve great taste.

Since many cooks enjoy making cakes from mixes, I have included many recipes in this section that begin with a convenient prepackaged mix. For these recipes, I modified favorite cake recipes, such as Cinnamon Swirl Cake, Strawberry Cake, and Key Lime Cake. Made with additions of tofu and pudding, these cakes are moist and always delicious. I've tested these recipes on dozens of people. They are frequent favorites.

NOTE: **Use low-fat silken tofu, 1% fat per serving in all recipes.**

Tip: *To reduce calories and increase nutrition, use fresh fruit and nonfat dessert topping between baked cake layers rather than frosting. For soy nutrition, replace regular dairy milk with soy milk. Soy milk makes a tender cake.*

APPLESAUCE CAKE

I like to top this lovely, high-rising, moist, tender cake with vanilla frosting.

2 cups applesauce
1/4 cup cooking oil
2 egg whites
3/4 cup tofu, drained and mashed
1 3/4 cups granulated sugar
1 3/4 cups unbleached all-purpose flour
2/3 cup soy flour
1½ teaspoons baking soda
1½ teaspoons salt
1 teaspoon cinnamon
1/2 teaspoon cloves
1/2 teaspoon allspice
1/2 teaspoon nutmeg
1/4 teaspoon baking powder
1 cup raisins
1/2 cup chopped walnuts (optional)

In large mixing bowl, beat together applesauce, oil, egg whites, and tofu 1 to 2 minutes. Mixture will be lumpy.

In separate small bowl, combine sugar, all-purpose flour, soy flour, baking soda, salt, cinnamon, cloves, allspice, nutmeg, and baking powder. Add to wet ingredients. Mix well. Fold in raisins and walnuts.

Preheat oven to 350°F. Spray two 9-inch cake pans with nonstick cooking spray. Divide batter between prepared cake pans. Bake 30 to 35 minutes. Let cool in pans. Ice with your favorite cream cheese or vanilla cream frosting or serve plain.

Yield: 16 servings

Nutrition Per Serving
Calories: 242
Total fat: 4.2 g
Cholesterol: 0
Carbohydrates: 48 g
Dietary fiber: 1.4 g
Protein: 5.3 g

Health Benefit:
Applesauce contains 28 IU of vitamin A but a mere 0.5 g of fat per one-cup serving.

SOUR CREAM DEVIL'S FOOD BUNDT CAKE

Sour cream and chocolate go hand-in-hand for a mouth-watering combination.

1 package (18.25 ounces) reduced-fat chocolate cake mix
1 package (4 servings) instant chocolate pudding mix
4 egg whites
1 cup nonfat milk
1 package (12.3 ounces) tofu, drained and mashed
1/2 cup light sour cream

In large mixing bowl, combine cake mix, dry pudding mix, egg whites, milk, tofu, and sour cream. Beat 1 to 2 minutes.

Preheat oven to 350°F. Spray a bundt pan with nonstick cooking spray. Spoon in batter. Bake 45 to 50 minutes or until a toothpick inserted into center comes out clean. Cool in pan 10 minutes. Remove to wire rack.

When cake has completely cooled, drizzle top with vanilla or chocolate glaze, if desired.

Yield: 12 servings

Nutrition Per Serving
Calories: 148
Total fat: 3.2 g
Cholesterol: 2 mg
Carbohydrates: 38 g
Dietary fiber: 1 g
Protein: 4.9 g

Health Benefit: Tofu contains vitamin E, an antioxidant that some research suggests may aid in preventing some heart disease and aging.

APPLE CAKE

Apple-ly rich, this is the best lower-fat apple cake I've ever tasted.

2 cups granulated sugar
6 egg whites
1 large egg
1/2 cup light butter
2 1/3 cups unbleached all-purpose flour
2/3 cup soy flour
1/2 teaspoon baking soda
1 teaspoon salt
1 teaspoon cinnamon
3 cups diced apples
1 teaspoon vanilla
1/2 cup pecans (optional)

In medium mixing bowl, beat together sugar, egg whites, egg, and butter.

In separate bowl, combine all-purpose flour, soy flour, baking soda, salt, and cinnamon. Add to wet ingredients. Mix until well blended. Stir in apples, vanilla, and pecans.

Preheat oven to 325°F. Spray three 8-inch square pans with nonstick cooking spray. Divide batter among prepared pans. Bake 25 to 30 minutes or until a toothpick inserted in center comes out clean. Cool in pans. Remove to wire racks.

Yield: 16 servings

Nutrition Per Serving
Calories: 238
Total fat: 5.8 g
Cholesterol: 15 mg
Carbohydrates: 43 g
Dietary fiber: 1.1 g
Protein: 3.9 g

Health Benefit: One apple contains 2.7 g of dietary fiber, 54 IU of vitamin A, and 117 mg of potassium.

MISSOURI CAKE

This delicious cake was the first-place winner in the 1996 Missouri Soyfoods Contest. Reprinted by permission of the Missouri Soybean Merchandising Council, this recipe comes from Regina Ramsey of Puxico, Missouri.

CAKE
2 sticks light butter
1 cup water
4 tablespoons cocoa
2 cups granulated sugar
1 1/3 cups unbleached all-purpose flour
2/3 cup soy flour
1/2 teaspoon salt
1/2 teaspoon baking soda
2 eggs
1/2 cup light sour cream
1 teaspoon vanilla

TO PREPARE CAKE
Bring butter, water, and cocoa to a boil. Remove from heat.

In medium mixing bowl, combine sugar, all-purpose flour, soy flour, salt, and baking soda. Beat in cocoa mixture. Add eggs, sour cream, and vanilla.

Preheat oven to 350°F. Spray cookie sheet with nonstick cooking spray and lightly flour. Pour batter onto prepared pan. Bake 20 minutes.

Yield: 20 servings

Nutrition Per Serving:

Calories: 203
Total fat: 9.2 g
Cholesterol: 24 mg
Carbohydrates: 28 g
Dietary fiber: 0.7 g
Protein: 2.8 g

Health Benefit: Defatted soy flour contains only 1.2 g fat per one-cup serving, yet has 47 g of protein. It's also a good source of calcium, with a one-cup serving delivering a whopping 241 mg.

AMARETTO CHEESECAKE

If you love the flavor of amaretto, you'll love this cheesecake. Even though it has a few extra grams of fat, this version is far lower than other versions, which can contain up to 50 grams of fat per serving.

CRUST
1 1/2 cups reduced-fat chocolate wafers
1 1/2 tablespoons granulated sugar
2 tablespoons light butter
2 ounces chopped almonds (optional)

FILLING
1 package (12.3 ounces) **silken** tofu, drained and mashed
2 packages (8 ounces each) 1/3-less-fat cream cheese
1 1/2 cups granulated sugar
6 egg whites
1 egg
1/4 cup amaretto liqueur
2 tablespoons vanilla
1 tablespoon almond extract

To prepare crust, spray a springform pan with nonstick cooking spray. In food processor or blender, combine chocolate wafers, sugar, butter, and almonds. Mix well. Press mixture into bottom and sides of pan.

Using food processor or blender, process tofu until smooth. With machine running, add cream cheese, one-quarter package at a time, processing thoroughly after each addition.

Add sugar, egg whites, egg, amaretto, vanilla, and almond extract, processing approximately 4 to 5 minutes or until mixture is velvety smooth. To ensure even mixing, stop machine from time to time and scrape sides of container. Thorough mixing is important to prevent cream cheese from lumping.

Preheat oven to 300°F. Pour mixture over crust. Bake 1 hour and 15 minutes. Cool in pan. Refrigerate for several hours or overnight to mellow flavor before serving.

Yield: 14 servings

Nutrition Per Serving
Calories: 330
Total fat: 9.9 g
Cholesterol: 24 mg
Carbohydrates: 57 g
Dietary fiber: 0.8 g
Protein: 4.6 g

Health Benefit: Tofu is an excellent source of phytochemicals and protein.

RAZZLE-DAZZLE RASPBERRY CHEESECAKE

This lower-fat cheesecake is wonderfully rich and creamy.

CRUST
1 cup fine graham-cracker crumbs
2 tablespoons granulated sugar
2 tablespoons light butter

FILLING
1 cup **silken** tofu, drained and mashed
1 package (8 ounces) 1/3-less-fat cream cheese, softened
1 package (8 ounces) fat-free cream cheese, softened
1 1/2 cups granulated sugar
1 cup reduced-fat sour cream
4 egg whites
1 teaspoon vanilla extract

RED RASPBERRY SAUCE
1 cup frozen unsweetened raspberries
3/4 cup granulated sugar
2 tablespoons cornstarch
1 cup plus 1 tablespoon water

To prepare crust, spray a springform pan with nonstick cooking spray. With a fork, mix cracker crumbs, sugar, and butter. Press mixture into bottom and sides of pan.

Using food processor or blender, process tofu until smooth. With machine running, add cream cheese, one-quarter package at a time, processing thoroughly after each addition. Add sugar, sour cream, egg whites, and vanilla, processing about 4 to 5 minutes or until mixture is velvety smooth. To ensure even mixing, stop machine from time to time and scrape sides of container. Thorough mixing is important to prevent cream cheese from lumping.

Preheat oven to 350°F. Pour mixture over crust. Bake 35 minutes. Turn off heat, leaving cheesecake in oven 1 hour. DO NOT OPEN OVEN DOOR. Cool in pan. Refrigerate several hours or overnight to mellow flavor. When ready to serve, spoon Red Raspberry Sauce over top.

TO PREPARE RED RASPBERRY SAUCE
In a heavy saucepan and over medium heat, bring berries, sugar, cornstarch, and water to a boil. Stir constantly until mixture thickens. Reduce heat and simmer 5 minutes.

Remove from heat. Refrigerate until cold. Spoon sauce over top of cheesecake.

Tip: Red Raspberry Sauce can be made ahead and stored in refrigerator up to 10 days.

Yield: 14 servings

Nutrition Per Serving
Calories: 260
Total fat: 6.4 g
Cholesterol: 21 mg
Carbohydrate: 46.1 g
Dietary fiber: 0.6 g
Protein: 5.2 g

Health Benefit: Tofu is packed with protein in a wonderful low-fat form.

GOLDEN THREE LAYER CAKE

An easy dessert idea, this light, tender cake is made with a prepackaged mix.

1 package (18.25 ounces) reduced-fat yellow cake mix
1 package (4 servings) vanilla instant pudding
4 egg whites
1 cup nonfat milk
1 package (12.3 ounce box) tofu, drained and mashed

In large mixing bowl, combine cake mix, dry pudding mix, egg whites, milk, and tofu. Beat 1 to 2 minutes.

Preheat oven to 350°F. Spray three 8-inch round cake pans with nonstick cooking spray. Divide batter among prepared pans. Bake 25 to 30 minutes or until a toothpick inserted into center comes out clean. Cool in pans 10 minutes. Remove to wire rack to finish cooling. When completely cool, frost with icing of your choice.

Yield: 12 servings

Nutrition Per Serving
Calories: 195
Total fat: 1.6 g
Cholesterol: 1 mg
Carbohydrates: 41 g
Dietary fiber: 0
Protein: 4.7 g

> **Health Benefit:** Tofu makes this cake moist and rich without adding additional fat. Tofu is also rich in B vitamins.

TROPICAL KEY LIME CAKE

Cool, light, and delicious, this cake is sure to please.

1 package (18.25 ounces) key lime cake mix
1 package (4 servings) pistachio instant pudding
4 egg whites
1 cup nonfat milk
1 package (12.3 ounce box) tofu, drained and mashed

In large mixing bowl, combine cake mix, dry pudding mix, egg whites, milk, and tofu. Beat 1 to 2 minutes.

Preheat oven to 350°F. Spray three 8-inch round cake pans with nonstick cooking spray. Divide batter among prepared pans. Bake 25 to 30 minutes or until a toothpick inserted into center comes out clean. Cool cake in pans 10 minutes. Remove to wire rack to finish cooling. When completely cool, frost with nonfat whipped topping.

Yield: 12 servings

Nutrition Per Serving
Calories: 195
Total fat: 4.8 g
Cholesterol: 1 mg
Carbohydrates: 41 g
Dietary fiber: 0
Protein: 4.7 g

Health Benefit: One slice of this cake has more protein than 4 ounces of milk.

STRAWBERRY DELIGHT CAKE

Layered with fresh strawberries, this light moist cake is good any time of the year.

1 package (18.25 ounces) reduced-fat strawberry cake mix
1 package (4 servings) vanilla instant pudding
4 egg whites
1 cup nonfat milk
1 package (12.3 ounce box) tofu, drained and mashed
1 quart sliced strawberries
2 packages nonfat dessert topping prepared with nonfat milk

In large mixing bowl, combine cake mix, dry pudding mix, egg whites, milk, and tofu. Beat 1 to 2 minutes.

Preheat oven to 350°F. Spray three 8-inch round cake pans with nonstick cooking spray. Divide batter among prepared pans. Bake 25 to 30 minutes or until a toothpick inserted into center comes out clean. Cool in pans 10 minutes. Remove to wire rack to finish cooling. When completely cool, frost each layer with prepared dessert topping. Top with sliced strawberries. Frost top and sides with prepared dessert topping. Decorate top with remaining strawberries.

Yield: 12 servings

Nutrition Per Serving
Calories: 195
Total fat: 1.6 g
Cholesterol: 1 mg
Carbohydrates: 41 g
Dietary fiber: 1 g
Protein: 4.7 g

Health Benefit: With strawberries and tofu, this cake is enriched with antioxidants and phytochemicals. Now, you can have your cake and eat it too!

CINNAMON SWIRL BUNDT CAKE

Filled with fragrant cinnamon, this delicious treat imitates the kind you (or Grandma) used to make, yet fat is reduced.

1 package (18.25 ounces) reduced-fat yellow cake mix
1 package (4 servings) instant vanilla pudding mix
4 egg whites
1 cup nonfat milk
1 box (12.3 ounces) tofu, drained and mashed
1/4 cup granulated sugar
1/2 teaspoon cinnamon

In large mixing bowl, combine cake mix, dry pudding mix, egg whites, milk, and tofu. Beat 1 to 2 minutes.

Preheat oven to 350°F. Spray a bundt pan with nonstick cooking spray. Pour in half of the batter.

Combine sugar and cinnamon. Sprinkle over batter in cake pan. Top with remaining batter.

Bake 45 to 50 minutes or until a toothpick inserted into center comes out clean. Cool cakes in pan. Remove to wire rack to finish cooling.

Yield: 12 servings

Nutrition Per Serving
Calories: 195
Total fat: 1.6 g
Cholesterol: 1 g
Carbohydrates: 41 g
Dietary fiber: 0
Protein: 4.7 g

Health Benefit: Tofu keeps the fat content of this cake low while keeping it moist and delicious.

SUNSHINE DUMP CAKE

Based on an old favorite recipe, this fruit-filled cake is bound to be a hit with family and friends.

3 bananas, sliced
1 can (8 ounces) crushed pineapple, undrained
1 can (11 ounces) mandarin oranges, undrained
1 package (18.25 ounces) yellow cake mix
1 package (6 servings) instant vanilla pudding mix
1 cup tofu, drained and mashed
1 cup fat-free evaporated milk

Preheat oven to 350°F. Spray 9 x 13-inch cake pan with nonstick cooking spray. Line bottom of pan with sliced bananas, pineapple and oranges (including juices).

In large bowl, beat cake mix, dry pudding mix, tofu, and milk. Mixture will be slightly thick. Spoon over fruit.

Bake 38 to 46 minutes or until a toothpick inserted into the center comes out clean. Cool and serve in pan.

Yield: 12 servings

Nutrition Per Serving
Calories: 200
Total fat: 4.8 g
Cholesterol: 2 mg
Carbohydrates: 36 g
Dietary fiber: 0.6 g
Protein: 4.5 g

Health Benefit: Pineapple is low in calories and high in vitamin A, with a one-cup serving supplying 1330 IU of this important vitamin.

Special Occasion Cakes

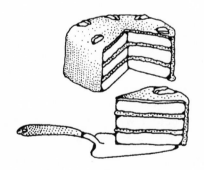

FESTIVE GINGERBREAD CAKE

Nothing fills the house with a warm, spicy aroma better than gingerbread. Knowing that this cake is lower in fat than traditional gingerbread cake, you'll love it even more.

2 tablespoons molasses
1/4 cup cooking oil
1/2 cup tofu, drained and mashed
1 egg
1 3/4 cups unbleached all-purpose flour
1/2 cup soy flour
1 1/2 cups granulated sugar
1 teaspoon ginger
1 teaspoon cinnamon
1/4 teaspoon cloves
1/2 teaspoon salt
1 teaspoon baking soda
1 teaspoon baking powder
1 tablespoon lemon juice
1 1/4 cups nonfat milk

In large mixing bowl, beat molasses, oil, tofu, and egg 1 to 2 minutes. Mixture will be lumpy.

Combine all-purpose flour, soy flour, sugar, ginger, cinnamon, cloves, salt, baking soda, and baking powder. Add to wet ingredients. Stir in lemon juice and milk. Beat until well blended.

Preheat oven to 350°F. Spray two 9-inch cake pans with nonstick cooking spray. Add batter. Bake 30 to 35 minutes. Cool in pans. Frost with your favorite icing or with nondairy dessert topping mix.

Yield: 16 servings

Nutrition Per Serving
Calories: 188
Total fat: 4.2 g
Cholesterol: 12 mg
Carbohydrates: 34 g
Dietary fiber: 0.6 g
Protein: 4.6 g

Health Benefit: Molasses is rich in calcium, with one cup of blackstrap molasses containing 176 mg of this bone builder.

CHOCOLATE ZUCCHINI CAKE

Vegetables have long been added to cakes and cookies. Here, zucchini combines with tofu to make a wonderfully rich, moist chocolate cake. Your kids won't fuss over eating these vegetables.

CAKE
1/2 cup light butter
1/2 cup tofu, drained and mashed
1 3/4 cups granulated sugar
1/2 cup egg substitute
1/2 cup low-fat buttermilk
2 teaspoons vanilla extract
2 1/2 cups unbleached all-purpose flour
4 tablespoons cocoa
1/2 teaspoon baking powder
1/2 teaspoon salt
2 teaspoons cloves
2 1/2 cups grated zucchini
1/4 cup baby food prunes
1 cup reduced-fat chocolate chips

TOPPING
1 cup plus 3 tablespoons reduced-fat chocolate chips
1/2 cup chopped walnuts (optional)
1/4 cup granulated sugar

In large mixing bowl, beat butter, tofu, and sugar until well blended. Mixture will be beady. Add egg substitute, buttermilk, and vanilla, beating well.

Combine all-purpose flour, cocoa, baking powder, salt, and cloves. Add to wet ingredients, beating 1 to 2 minutes. Stir in zucchini, baby food prunes, and chocolate chips.

Preheat oven to 325°F. Spray 9 x 13-inch cake pan with nonstick cooking spray. Add batter. Bake 45 to 50 minutes or until a toothpick inserted in center comes out clean.

Combine chocolate chips, walnuts, and sugar. As soon as cake is removed from oven, frost with topping. Chocolate pieces will melt on cake.

Yield: 12 servings

Nutrition Per Serving
Calories: 400
Total fat: 10.9 g
Cholesterol: 21 mg
Carbohydrates: 58.8 g
Dietary fiber: 4.3 g
Protein: 7 g

Health Benefit: The lowly zucchini is a nutritious vegetable. A one-cup serving contains 1.5 g of fiber, 1.4 g of protein, 306 mg of potassium, 19 mg of calcium, 0.5 mg of iron, 0.3 mg of zinc, 420 IU of vitamin A, 27.3 mcg of folacin, plus traces of vitamin B1, B2, and niacin. Tofu slips in additional protein and calcium.

CHARLOTTE'S DECADENT CHOCOLATE CAKE

My sister Charlotte created this lovely lower-fat version of her favorite chocolate cake. This wonderfully rich dessert should be served on your most festive occasions.

CAKE
1 3/4 cups granulated sugar
1/4 cup tofu, drained and mashed
3/4 cup light butter
2 cups unbleached all-purpose flour
1/4 cup soy flour
3/4 cup cocoa
1 1/2 teaspoons baking soda
1 1/4 teaspoons baking powder
1 teaspoon salt
1/4 cup baby food prunes
3/4 cup plus 1 tablespoon nonfat milk
1 cup egg substitute
1 1/4 teaspoons vanilla extract

In large mixing bowl, beat sugar, tofu, and butter until creamy, about 2 to 3 minutes. Add all-purpose flour, soy flour, cocoa, baking soda, baking powder, salt, baby food prunes, milk, egg substitute, and vanilla. Beat 2 to 3 minutes or until well blended.

Preheat oven to 350°F. Spray three 9-inch cake pans with nonstick cooking spray. Add batter. Bake 25 to 30 minutes or until a toothpick inserted into the center comes out clean. Cool completely on wire racks. For a festive cake, prepare your favorite chocolate frosting.

For other occasions, serve plain or with nonfat dessert topping.

Yield: 16 serving

Nutrition Per Serving
Calories: 244
Total fat: 9.1 g
Cholesterol: 23 mg
Carbohydrates: 37.7g
Dietary fiber: 2.1g
Protein: 5.1 g

Health Benefit: Soy flour and tofu add a double calcium boost to this recipe.

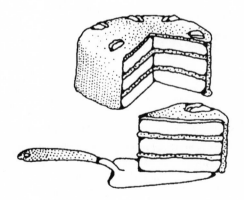

HAWAIIAN ISLE CAKE

Made from a whole-wheat cake mix, this luscious dessert is perfect for anyone wanting some nutrition from a sweet treat.

CAKE
1 cup brown sugar, packed
1/2 cup tofu, drained and mashed
2 tablespoons baby food prunes
1 1/2 teaspoons cooking oil
1/4 cup plus 3 tablespoons nonfat milk
2 tablespoons reserved pineapple juice
1 package whole wheat banana snack cake mix (12.5 ounces)
3 egg whites
1 teaspoon cream of tartar
1/2 cup crushed pineapple, well drained (reserve liquid)
1/4 cup raisins
1/4 cup walnuts (optional)

TOPPING
1 package nonfat dessert topping mix, prepared with nonfat milk

FILLING
1/2 cup brown sugar, packed
1 1/2 tablespoons cornstarch
Pinch of salt
4 ounces (1/2 can) crushed pineapple, juice included
2 tablespoons water
1/4 cup plus 2 tablespoons egg substitute

TO PREPARE CAKE
In large mixing bowl, beat sugar, tofu, baby food prunes, oil, milk, and pineapple juice until well blended. Mixture will be beady. Stir in dry cake mix.

In a medium bowl, beat egg whites until they stand in soft peaks. Beat in cream of tartar. Fold in egg whites. Stir in pineapple, raisins, and walnuts. Preheat oven to 350°F. Spray two 8-inch cake pans with nonstick cooking spray and add batter. Bake 25 to 28 minutes. Cool in pans. Remove to wire racks.

TO PREPARE FILLING AND ASSEMBLE CAKE

In medium saucepan, combine sugar, cornstarch, a pinch of salt, pineapple, including juice, and water. Bring mixture to boil over medium heat, stirring constantly. Remove from heat. Add egg substitute, beating well. Bring to a boil again, stirring constantly. Boil 1 minute. Remove from heat and cool.

To assemble cake, place one layer (top side down) on large cake plate. Spread with filling. Repeat with second layer. Top with nonfat dessert topping mix. Keep refrigerated until ready to serve.

Yield: 16 servings

Nutrition Per Serving

Calories: 210
Total fat: 3.3 g
Cholesterol: 0 mg
Carbohydrates: 50 g
Dietary fiber: 0.3 g
Protein: 2.3 g

Health Benefit: Per one-cup serving, pineapple contains 27 mcg of folacin plus traces of other B vitamins.

COCONUT CAKE WITH LIME FILLING

Cool as an ocean breeze, this delicious cake reduces the fat and cholesterol of the original version (which called for six eggs and a whipped cream filling!) while retaining the flavor.

CAKE
1/2 cup tofu, drained and mashed
1/2 cup light butter
2 cups granulated sugar
5 egg whites
2 1/2 cup unbleached all-purpose flour
2 1/2 teaspoons baking powder
1/2 teaspoon salt
1 cup nonfat milk
1 1/2 teaspoons vanilla extract

TOPPING
1 package nonfat dessert topping mix
2 to 3 tablespoons grated coconut
4 to 5 thin slices of lime

FILLING
1 cup plus 2 tablespoons granulated sugar
3 tablespoons cornstarch
1/4 teaspoon salt
1/2 cup diluted orange juice
1 tablespoon lemon juice
3 tablespoons lime juice
1/4 cup water
3/4 cup egg substitute
1 tablespoon grated lemon peel
1 tablespoon grated lime peel

TO PREPARE CAKE

In large mixing bowl, thoroughly beat tofu, butter, and sugar 1 to 2 minutes or until creamy. In medium bowl, beat egg whites until soft peaks form. Set aside.

Combine all-purpose flour, baking powder, and salt. Add to wet ingredients. Stir in milk and vanilla. Beat 1 to 2 minutes or until well blended. Fold in egg whites.

Preheat oven to 350°F. Spray three 8-inch cake pans with nonstick cooking spray. Divide batter evenly among pans. Bake 30 to 35 minutes or until a toothpick inserted into center comes out clean. Cool in pans. Remove to wire racks.

TO PREPARE FILLING AND ASSEMBLE CAKE

In small saucepan, mix sugar, cornstarch, and salt. Stir in juices and water. Bring to a boil over medium heat, stirring constantly. Remove from heat. Add egg substitute, beating well. Bring to boil again, stirring constantly, boiling 1 minute. Remove from heat. Stir in lemon and lime peels. Pour into a bowl. Cool over ice water.

To assemble cake, place one layer top side down on a large cake plate. Spread with half of filling mixture. Repeat with second layer and remainder of filling. Place top layer right side up. Prepare nonfat dessert topping mix according to package directions. Frost sides and top. Sprinkle with coconut. Arrange 5 or 6 lime slices in a decorative pattern in center of cake. Refrigerate until ready to serve.

Yield: 16 servings

Nutrition Per Serving

Calories: 314
Total fat: 6.7 g
Cholesterol: 15 mg
Carbohydrates: 71.5 g
Dietary fiber: 0.8 g
Protein: 4.2 g

Health Benefit: Per one-cup serving, lime juice contains 20.2 mcg of folacin and 268 mg potassium.

LUSCIOUS LEMON POPPY SEED CAKE

This old-time favorite makes a four-layer cake that is perfect for large gatherings. Our version is dressed up with fresh blueberries for an even tastier—and more nutritious—celebration.

CAKE
2 packages (12.5 ounces each) fat-free or reduced-fat lemon
  snack cake mix
1 cup egg substitute
1 package (4.3 ounces) cook-and-serve lemon pudding mix
2 tablespoons soy flour
2 cups nonfat milk
1/2 cup tofu, drained and mashed
6 tablespoons poppy seeds
1/2 teaspoon grated orange peel

TOPPING
1 package nonfat dessert topping mix
1 3/4 cups frozen blueberries
Confectioners sugar

LEMON CURD
1/2 cup lemon juice
1 cup granulated sugar
1/4 cup light butter
2 egg yolks
1/2 cup egg substitute

TO PREPARE CAKE
In large mixing bowl, beat dry cake mix, egg substitute, dry pudding mix, soy flour, milk, and tofu 1 to 2 minutes, or until creamy. Stir in poppy seeds and orange peel.

Preheat oven to 350°F. Spray two 9-inch cake pans with nonstick cooking spray. Divide batter evenly between pans. Bake 25 to

30 minutes or until a toothpick inserted into center comes out clean. Cool in pans 10 to 15 minutes. Remove to wire racks.

TO PREPARE LEMON CURD AND ASSEMBLE CAKE

In a large saucepan, whisk lemon juice, sugar, butter, egg yolks, and egg substitute until well combined. Cook over medium heat, stirring constantly with a wooden spoon. Cook about 30 to 35 minutes or until curd thickens and reduces in volume. Scrape sides of saucepan to prevent burning. Remove from heat and cool.

When cake has completely cooled, split layers horizontally with a serrated knife. Place one layer cut side down on a serving platter. Spread 1/2 cup lemon curd, covering to edge of cake. Top with 1/4 cup blueberries. Place second layer on top of first. Spread with another 1/2 cup of lemon curd. Top with another 1/4 cup blueberries. Repeat process with third layer. **Tip:** *The layers can be prepared ahead of time and kept covered and refrigerated until ready to serve.*

When ready to serve, prepare nonfat dessert topping mix, using nonfat milk.

Place final layer atop cake. Spread with nonfat dessert topping mix, using entire package. Sprinkle with remaining 1 cup of blueberries. Dust cake lightly with confectioners sugar. Keep refrigerated.

Yield: 16 servings

Nutrition Per Serving

Calories: 351
Total fat: 5.8 g
Cholesterol: 8 mg
Carbohydrates: 78.4 g
Dietary fiber: 1.4 g
Protein: 6.8 g

Health Benefit: A one-cup serving of blueberries contains 3.8 g of dietary fiber, 126 mg of potassium, and 9 mg of calcium.

BANANA-FILLED SOUR CREAM CAKE

You'll want to serve this elegant, moist, and simply delicious cake often.

CAKE
2 packages (12.5 oz.) fat-free or reduced fat banana cake mix
1 cup egg substitute
1 package (4.3 oz.) cook-and-serve banana pudding mix
2 tablespoons soy flour
2 cups nonfat milk
1/2 cup tofu, drained and mashed

TOPPINIG
1 package fluffy white frosting mix, prepared according to directions

FILLING
2 tablespoons light butter
1/3 cup brown sugar, packed
3 pounds bananas, sliced
Poppy seeds
1 1/2 cups light sour cream

TO PREPARE CAKE
In large mixing bowl, beat together dry cake mix, egg substitute, dry pudding mix, soy flour, milk, and tofu until well blended.

Preheat oven to 350°F. Spray two 9-inch cake pans with nonstick cooking spray. Divide batter evenly between pans. Bake 30 to 35 minutes or until a toothpick inserted into the center comes out clean. Cool 10 to 15 minutes in pans. Remove to wire racks.

TO PREPARE FILLING AND ASSEMBLE CAKE

Over medium heat, combine butter and brown sugar in a skillet, stirring until sugar dissolves. Add bananas, cooking just until tender. Stir mixture gently with a fork. Remove from heat. Let cool until ready to assemble cake.

When cake is completely cool, split layers horizontally with a serrated knife. Place one layer cut side down on serving platter. Evenly spread with 1/2 cup sour cream. Top with 1/3 of banana filling.

Repeat process with second and third layers.

When ready to serve, prepare frosting. Place final layer on cake. Ice top and sides with frosting mix. Sprinkle top with poppy seeds. Serve immediately. Refrigerate leftovers.

Yield: 16 serving

Nutrition Per Serving
Calories: 331
Total fat: 3.3 g
Cholesterol: 6 mg
Carbohydrates: 73 g
Dietary fiber: 1 g
Protein: 5.3 g

Health Benefit: Bananas add vitamins and fiber to your diet. Bananas contain potassium, 60 IU of vitamin A, 14.1 mcg of folacin, plus some calcium, iron, zinc, and B vitamins, including 0.68 mg of heart-healthy B6. Combined with the goodness of soy flour and tofu, this cake will provide energy while satisfying your sweet tooth.

* analysis per reduced fat cake mix

MOIST AND DELICIOUS BANANA LAYER CAKE

If you love bananas, you'll love this rich, easy-to-make cake.

1 package reduced-fat banana cake mix
1 cup egg substitute
1 package (4 servings) instant banana pudding mix
1 cup nonfat milk
1/2 cup tofu, drained and mashed

In mixing bowl, beat together dry cake mix, egg substitute, dry pudding mix, milk, and tofu, blending well.

Preheat oven to 350°F. Spray two 8- or 9-inch layer pans with nonstick cooking spray. Divide batter evenly between pans. Bake 30-35 minutes or until a toothpick inserted into center comes out clean. Top with your favorite frosting.

Yield: 16 servings

Nutrition Per Serving
Calories: 152
Total fat: 1.3 g
Cholesterol: 1 mg
Carbohydrates: 31 g
Dietary Fiber 0
Protein: 4.3 g

Health Benefit: One banana contains 60 IU of vitamin A and 14.1 mcg of folacin, along with potassium, some calcium, iron, zinc, and B vitamins, including 0.68 mg of heart-healthy B6.

FRESH CARROT CAKE

A whole new concept in cake baking, this delicious cake is a little higher in fat, but it is oh, so good.

2 eggs
4 egg whites
1/2 cup low-fat silken tofu, drained and mashed
1 can (8 oz.) crushed pineapple, undrained
1 cup granulated or milled sugar
1 cup brown sugar
1/2 teaspoon cinnamon
1/4 teaspoon cardamon
1/4 teaspoon nutmeg
2 cups all-purpose flour
2 teaspoons baking powder
2 taspoons baking soda
1 teaspoon salt
3 cups carrots, grated
1/2 cup cooking oil

Combine eggs, egg whites, oil, and tofu. Add pineapple. Mix dry ingredients. Add to wet ingredients. Add carrots.

Preheat oven to 350°F. Spray two 9-inch round cake pans with nonstick cooking spray. Pour in batter. Bake 35-45 minutes or until a toothpick inserted into center comes out clean. Cool in pans 10 minutes. Remove to wire rack to finish cooling. When completely cool, frost with icing of your choice.

Yield: 16 servings

Nutrition Per Serving
Calories: 252
Total fat: 10.7 g
Cholesterol: 23 mg
Carbohydrates: 42.5 g
Dietary fiber: 1.2 g
Protein: 4.2 g

Health Benefit: One cup of carrots contains only 42 calories and is rich in vitamin A.

LAGGTARTA

Stacked in five layers, oozing with strawberries and creamy filling, this cake is the perfect summertime treat.

3 egg whites
2 teaspoons white distilled vinegar
1 cup granulated sugar
1 cup cake flour, sifted
1 teaspoon baking powder
1/2 cup tofu, drained and mashed
1 cup lemon curd (see page 188)
3 cups strawberries, sliced
1 package nonfat dessert topping, made with nonfat milk

In deep bowl, beat egg whites until fluffy. Add vinegar and 1/2 cup sugar. Continue beating until soft peaks form. Add remaining 1/2 cup sugar. Beat until mixture reaches a soft consistency.

In large mixing bowl, sift together flour and baking powder. Slowly add egg whites to dry ingredients. Add tofu to batter. Beat well, 1 to 2 minutes.

Preheat oven to 425°F. Spray three 8-inch round cake pans with nonstick cooking spray. Pour 1/5 batter into each prepared pan. There will be a thin layer in each. Five thin layers are needed.

Bake 5 minutes. Cake will not be brown. Remove layers from pans. Wash and dry two pans. Spray with nonstick cooking spray. Fill these two pans with another thin layer of cake batter. Bake 5 minutes. Remove final layer from pans.

When cakes have completely cooled, spread first cake layer with a thin layer of lemon curd, a thin layer of sliced strawberries, and a thin layer of nonfat dessert topping mix. Stack with second cake layer. Spread with a thin layer of lemon curd, a thin layer of sliced strawberries, and a thin layer of nonfat dessert topping mix. Stack a third layer. Repeat process until all layers are used. Dollop dessert topping in middle of top layer. Decorate with whole strawberries. Refrigerate at least 6 hours.

When ready to serve, use an electric knife to slice into wedges. Serve with additional strawberries and nonfat dessert topping mix.

Yield: 14 servings

Nutrition Per Serving
Calories: 153
Total fat: 3 g
Cholesterol: 4 mg
Carbohydrates: 29.7 g
Dietary fiber: 0.8 g
Protein: 1.9 g

Health Benefit: Per cup, strawberries contain 233 mg of potassium, 20 mg of calcium, plus some iron, vitamins A and B, and traces of niacin.

Notes

Fabulous Pies

PIES

The secret of a scrumptious pie is a tender crust and a wonderfully sweet filling. Luscious pies add festive touches to tables. Even a pie that isn't picture perfect will be loved by all. When fruit is used in pies, the pie is richer in antioxidants.

Traditional piecrusts contain from 25 to 32 or more grams of fat per serving. Even though fat-free versions of crusts are available in some cookbooks, the ones I've tried are mainly tough and chewy. And since I'm palate driven and nutrition oriented, I wanted a reduced-fat crust with good taste and increased health benefits.

The reduced-fat piecrusts in this cookbook are both tasty and tender. They reduce two-thirds of the saturated fat found in shortening crust, and they are delicious. Oil easily replaces part of the shortening, and although oil is fat, if polyunsaturated or monounsaturated oil is used, this fat is considered, by most, to be healthier than saturated fat found in shortening. While the overall fat content in most of these crusts is 7 grams per serving, the fat is necessary to keep crust tender. If you don't tell your family and friends your baking secret, they won't know the difference between the soy crust and a more traditional crust.

To make soy piecrust, I generally use Soya Powder purchased from health food stores. This product contains 5 grams of fat per quarter-cup serving. Defatted soy flour contains 1.2 grams of fat per one-cup serving, but crust made with defatted soy flour will be less tender. Soya powder turns crust a golden color, while defatted soy flour produces a darker crust.

Soy flour and Soya powder provide additional protein, calcium, and minerals.

If you want to try using defatted soy flour, decrease the amount of ice water used in the piecrust, using only enough to bind the ingredients together. I have made good piecrust with defatted soy flour, but the texture was always a bit firm.

To further reduce fat in pies, just use a bottom layer of crust, and top off with a thin coating of streusel, a whisper of sugar, meringue, or nonfat dairy topping. Of course, plain is always a good choice for fruit pies. When you simply must have a top layer of crust, use a lattice of pie dough instead of a solid covering.

INNOVATIVE TECHNIQUES

Working with lower-fat piecrust calls for innovative methods of handling pastry dough. When making dough, heat butter and oil over low heat. Knead butter mixture into dough. Do not add additional flour. Dough will be softer than traditional higher-fat versions.

Wrap dough in plastic wrap. Refrigerate until well chilled, approximately 30 to 60 minutes. When ready to prepare, use plastic wrap to roll out crust. Do not add additional flour, which will make the crust tough. You can also flatten the pastry with your hand. Keep working the dough until it is the desired size.

IF YOU WANT TO MAKE PUDDING

To reduce fat from pie, serve pudding without the crust. For an easy nondairy pudding, try this easy recipe made with low-fat soy milk. This pudding can easily be served either with or without crust. If you want to serve pudding from a mix, you can purchase dry mixes at health food stores. Simply add tofu and blend. The texture is creamy smooth. The taste is great.

NONDAIRY VANILLA PUDDING

This pudding is perfect for those who are allergic to or prefer not to eat dairy products.

1 cup water
1 1/2 cups granulated sugar
1/2 cup cornstarch
1/4 teaspoon salt
3 cups low-fat soy milk
3 teaspoons vanilla extract

In 3-quart saucepan, combine water, sugar, cornstarch, and salt. Stir in soy milk, and bring mixture to a slow boil over medium heat, stirring constantly. When mixture thickens, lower heat and continue cooking another 3 to 5 minutes. Continue stirring. Do not let mixture burn.

Remove from heat. Stir in vanilla. Let cool. Serve as is, or when slightly cool, process in a food processor or blender until creamy smooth.

Yield: 8 servings

Nutrition Per Serving
Calories: 210
Total fat: 1.7 g
Cholesterol: 0
Carbohydrates: 47 g
Dietary fiber: 1.2 g
Protein: 2.5 g

Health Benefit: Plain, unfortified soy milk is an excellent source of high-quality protein. Some soy milk is fortified with additional vitamins like vitamin D and B-12, minerals, and is a good source of calcium.

BASIC TENDER LOWER-FAT PIECRUST

Moist, tender, and easy to make, this lower-fat crust will please even picky eaters.

3/4 cup plus 1 tablespoon unbleached all-purpose flour
3 tablespoons Soya powder
2 tablespoons granulated sugar
1/8 teaspoon salt
1 tablespoon cornstarch
2 tablespoons light butter
3 tablespoons cooking oil
2 tablespoons ice water

In medium bowl, combine all-purpose flour, Soya powder, sugar, salt, and cornstarch.

In small saucepan, melt butter over low heat. Add oil. Remove from heat. Carefully stir butter mixture into flour mixture with a fork. Mixture will be crumbly. Add ice water, 1 tablespoon at a time, adding just enough to make dough pliable and to bind dough. Knead lightly with fingers until dough is smooth and holds its shape. Wrap in plastic wrap. Refrigerate 30 to 60 minutes. Preheat oven to 400°F.

Coat a pie plate with nonstick cooking spray. Lay a sheet of plastic wrap on work surface. Place dough in center of plastic wrap. Cover with another sheet. Roll dough to 12-inch circle. Remove top layer of plastic. Carefully place rolled-out dough into prepared pie plate, pastry side down, gently pressing into bottom and sides. Discard remaining plastic. Prick dough with a fork. Line pastry shell with foil, covering edges. Fill with dried beans for weight.

Bake 10 minutes. Remove beans and foil. Bake dough 10 minutes longer or until crust is golden brown. Cool on wire rack.

Yield: 8 serving

Nutrition Per Serving
Calories: 137
Total fat: 8.4 g
Cholesterol: 8 mg
Carbohydrates: 13.4 g
Dietary fiber: 0.6 g
Protein: 2 g

Health Benefit: Soya powder is protein rich.

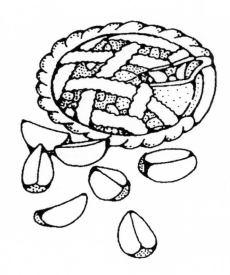

SPICED APPLE-RAISIN CRISSCROSS

Apple-ly rich, raisin-y good, and simply delicious.

PIECRUST
1 1/2 cups plus 2 tablespoons unbleached all-purpose flour
6 tablespoons Soya powder
3 tablespoons granulated sugar
1/4 teaspoon salt
2 tablespoons cornstarch
1/2 teaspoon cinnamon
1 tablespoon finely grated orange peel
4 tablespoons unsalted light butter
6 tablespoons cooking oil
3-4 tablespoons ice water

FILLING
4 cups thinly sliced apples
1/2 cup granulated sugar
1 teaspoon cinnamon
1 tablespoon cornstarch

TO PREPARE PIECRUST
In medium mixing bowl, combine all-purpose flour, Soya powder, sugar, salt, cornstarch, cinnamon, and orange peel.

In small saucepan, melt butter over low heat. Add oil. Remove from heat. Using a fork, carefully stir butter mixture into flour mixture. Mixture will be crumbly. Add ice water, 1 tablespoon at a time, adding just enough to make dough pliable and to bind dough.

Knead lightly with fingers until dough is smooth and holds its shape. Wrap in plastic wrap. Refrigerate 30 to 60 minutes.

When dough is ready, lay a sheet of plastic wrap on work surface. Place two-thirds of dough in center, reserving remainding dough for a lattice top. Cover with another sheet of plastic wrap. Roll dough to 14 x 10-inch oblong.

Coat a 13 x 9-inch baking dish with nonstick cooking spray. Remove top layer of plastic wrap. Carefully place rolled-out dough into prepared baking dish, pastry side down. Gently press dough into bottom and about 1/2 to 1 inch up sides. Discard remaining plastic.

TO PREPARE FILLING
Preheat oven to 400°F. Spread sliced apples over piecrust. Sprinkle with water. Sprinkle sugar, cinnamon, and cornstarch over apples.

Roll out remaining dough. Cut into 1/2 inch wide strips. Crisscross strips over filling to form lattice.

Bake 10 minutes. Reduce oven heat to 375°F degrees. Bake 20 minutes longer or until pastry is golden brown.

Yield: 16 servings

Nutrition Per Serving
Calories: 168
Total fat: 7.2 g
Cholesterol: 8 mg
Carbohydrates: 24 g
Dietary fiber: 1 g
Protein: 2 g

Health Benefit: Apples are rich in fiber, with 1 1/4 cups containing 3.4 g. They also contain 7 g of vitamin C, 67 IU vitamin A, and 3.6 mcg of folacin.

CRAN-APPLE STRUDEL

Strudel has been around a long time, yet traditional recipes can be laden with butter and high in fat. This lower-fat version allows the flavor of the apples to seep through.

PIECRUST
1 Tender Lower-fat Piecrust (see index)

FILLING
6 medium apples, coarsely chopped
1/2 cup granulated sugar
1/4 cup dried cranberries
3/4 cup brown sugar, packed
2 cups water
1/2 teaspoon cinnamon
1/2 tablespoon cornstarch

TO PREPARE PIECRUST
Prepare piecrust dough according to recipe instructions.

When dough is ready, lay a sheet of plastic wrap on work surface. Place dough in center. Cover with another sheet of plastic wrap. Roll to 11 x 9-inch oblong. Coat 13 x 9-inch baking dish with nonstick cooking spray. Remove top layer of plastic wrap. Carefully place rolled-out dough into prepared baking dish, pastry side down. Discard remaining plastic.

TO PREPARE FILLING
Preheat oven to 350°F. In medium bowl, combine apples, granulated sugar, and cranberries. Spoon mixture down the middle of dough. Gently fold both sides up around the filling, barely overlapping top edges. Pinch ends together to seal.

Bring brown sugar, water, cinnamon, and cornstarch to a boil. Pour over pastry. Bake 50 to 55 minutes. Remove and cut into 1-inch slices. Serve warm. Refrigerate leftover portions.

Yield: 11 servings

Nutrition Per Serving
Calories: 229
Total fat: 5.4 g
Cholesterol: 6 mg
Carbohydrates: 45 g
Dietary fiber: 2 g
Protein: 2 g

Health Benefit: Aside from fiber and vitamin content, apples contain pectin, which many believe aids in lowering cholesterol.

COLONIAL PUMPKIN PIE

This Thanksgiving standard is based on my mother's recipe. Like the original, this soy version is rich with dark, sweet molasses and generously flavored with spice.

PIECRUST
1 Tender Lower-fat Piecrust (see index)

FILLING
1 package silken tofu (12.3 ounces) drained and mashed
1 can (16 ounces) pumpkin
1 cup brown sugar, packed
1 teaspoon ginger
1 teaspoon cinnamon
1/8 teaspoon allspice
2 tablespoons molasses
2 egg whites, beaten
1 egg
1 cup low-fat soy milk

TO PREPARE PIECRUST
Prepare piecrust dough according to recipe instructions.

Coat pie plate with nonstick cooking spray. Remove top layer of plastic wrap from dough. Carefully place dough into prepared pie plate, pastry side down. Gently press into the bottom and sides. Discard remaining plastic.

TO PREPARE FILLING
Preheat oven to 425°F. Using a food processor or blender, process tofu until creamy. Spoon into a large mixing bowl. Add pumpkin, sugar, ginger, cinnamon, allspice, molasses, egg whites, egg, and soy milk. Mix ingredients thoroughly. Pour into unbaked pie shell. Bake 15 minutes. Reduce heat to 350°F. Bake 40 minutes longer or until a knife inserted in center comes out clean.

Yield: 8 servings

Nutrition Per Serving
Calories: 276
Total fat: 8.4 g
Cholesterol: 8 mg
Carbohydrates: 48.6 g
Dietary fiber: 1.7 g
Protein: 2.8 g

Health Benefit: Pumpkin, a member of the squash family, is an excellent source of potassium, with one cup containing 504 mg. It also contains a whopping 5,404 mg of vitamin A, 64 mg of calcium, 56 mg of magnesium, and a host of other vitamins and minerals.

DEEP-DISH RAISIN APPLE PIE

Thick layers of apples and raisins make this pie delectable. This version brings home childhood memories of Mom's pies while reducing some of the less memorable fat.

PIECRUST
1 1/2 cups plus 2 tablespoons unbleached all-purpose flour
6 tablespoons Soya powder
3 tablespoons granulated sugar
1/4 teaspoon salt
2 tablespoons cornstarch
4 tablespoons light butter
6 tablespoons cooking oil
3 to 4 tablespoons ice water

FILLING
6 cups apples, peeled and chopped
3/4 cup golden raisins
1/4 cup sliced almonds (optional)
3/4 cup brown sugar, packed
1/2 cup undiluted apple juice concentrate
1 tablespoon lemon juice
1/4 teaspoon lemon zest
1 teaspoon cinnamon
1/8 teaspoon cloves
1/4 teaspoon salt

TO PREPARE PIECRUST
In medium mixing bowl, combine all-purpose flour, Soya powder, sugar, salt, and cornstarch.

In small saucepan, melt butter over low heat. Add cooking oil. Remove from heat. Carefully stir butter mixture into flour mixture with a fork. Mixture will be crumbly. Add ice water, 1 tablespoon at a time, adding just enough to make dough pliable and to bind dough. Knead lightly with fingers until dough is smooth and holds its shape. Wrap in plastic wrap. Refrigerate 30 to 60 minutes.

When dough is ready, lay a sheet of plastic wrap on work surface. Place two-thirds of the dough in center, reserving remainder for lattice top. Cover with another sheet of plastic wrap. Roll dough to 14 x 10-inch oblong.

Coat 13 x 9-inch oblong baking dish with nonstick cooking spray. Remove top layer of plastic wrap. Carefully place rolled-out dough into prepared baking dish, pastry side down. Gently press dough into bottom of dish and about ½ to 1 inch up sides. Discard remaining plastic.

TO PREPARE FILLING AND ASSEMBLE PIE
Preheat oven to 350°F. In large bowl, combine apples, raisins, almonds, sugar, apple juice, lemon juice, lemon zest, cinnamon, cloves, and salt. Pour into piecrust.

Roll out remaining pastry. Cut into ½ inch wide strips. Crisscross strips over filling to form a lattice. Cover edges with a 2-inch strip of aluminum foil to prevent excessive browning. Bake 55 to 60 minutes.

Yield: 8 servings

Nutrition Per Serving
Calories: 446
Total fat: 17.1 g
Cholesterol: 15 mg
Carbohydrates: 71.2 g
Dietary fiber: 4 g
Protein: 4.7 g

Health Benefit: Spices spark up nutrition. One tablespoon of cinnamon contains 34 mg of potassium, 84 mg of calcium, 2.6 mg of iron, 2 mg of vitamin C, 81 IU of vitamin A, and traces of several B vitamins.

DEEP-DISH BLUEBERRY PIE

Filled to the rim with bright blueberries, this fruit-and-juice pie rates the rave reviews it always gets.

PIECRUST
1 1/4 cups unbleached all-purpose flour
1/4 cup Soya powder
3 tablespoons granulated sugar
1/4 teaspoon salt
1 1/2 tablespoons cornstarch
3 tablespoons light butter
1/4 cup cooking oil
3 tablespoons ice water

FILLING
1 cup brown sugar, packed
1 teaspoon lemon zest
1/8 teaspoon salt
1 package (16 ounces) frozen blueberries
1 teaspoon lemon juice
1 tablespoon soy flour
2 tablespoon cornstarch
2 tablespoons turbinado sugar (optional)

TO PREPARE PIECRUST
In medium mixing bowl, combine all-purpose flour, Soya powder, sugar, salt, and cornstarch.

In small saucepan, melt butter over low heat. Add oil. Remove from heat. Carefully stir butter mixture into flour mixture with a fork. The mixture will be crumbly. Add ice water, 1 tablespoon at a time, adding just enough to make dough pliable and to bind dough. Knead lightly with fingers until dough is smooth and holds its shape. Wrap in plastic wrap. Refrigerate 30 to 60 minutes.

When dough is ready, lay a sheet of plastic wrap on work surface Place three-quarters of dough in center, reserving remainder for a lattice top. Cover with another sheet of plastic wrap. Roll dough to 12-inch circle.

Coat a pie plate with nonstick cooking spray. Remove top layer of plastic wrap. Carefully place rolled-out dough into prepared pie plate, pastry side down. Gently press dough into bottom and sides of pie plate. Discard remaining plastic.

TO PREPARE FILLING AND ASSEMBLE PIE
Preheat oven to 350°F. In large bowl, combine sugar, lemon zest, salt, blueberries, lemon juice, soy flour, and cornstarch. Pour mixture into pastry shell.

Roll out remaining dough. Cut into 1/2 inch wide strips. Crisscross strips over filling to form lattice. Sprinkle with turbinado sugar, if desired. Cover edges with 2-inch strip of aluminum foil to prevent excessive browning. Bake 60 to 65 minutes or until golden brown.

Yield: 8 servings

Nutrition Per Serving
Calories: 348
Total fat: 11.8 g
Cholesterol: 11 mg
Carbohydrates: 58.3 g
Dietary fiber: 2.6 g
Protein: 3.8 g

Health Benefit: A cup of raw blueberries contains 9 mg of calcium, 0.2 mg of iron, 126 mg of potassium, and 0.2 mg of zinc, as well as vitamin C and minerals such as thiamin, riboflavin, niacin, and folate.

DEEP-DISH SOUTHERN CHERRY PIE

Tart, refreshing, a springtime delight, this pie will win ribbons of praise every time.

PIECRUST
1 1/4 cups unbleached all-purpose flour
1/4 cup Soya powder
3 tablespoons granulated sugar
1/4 teaspoon salt
1 1/2 tablespoons cornstarch
3 tablespoons light butter
1/4 cup cooking oil
3 tablespoons ice water

FILLING
1 cup water
1 cup granulated sugar
1 package (16 ounces) frozen cherries, pitted
1/4 cup unbleached all-purpose flour
1/2 teaspoon cinnamon
1 tablespoon soy flour
3 tablespoons turbinado sugar

TO PREPARE PIECRUST
In medium mixing bowl, combine all-purpose flour, Soya powder, sugar, salt, and cornstarch.

In small saucepan, melt butter over low heat. Add oil. Remove from heat. Carefully stir butter mixture into flour mixture with a fork. Mixture will be crumbly. Add ice water, 1 tablespoon at a time, adding just enough to make dough pliable and to bind dough. Knead lightly with fingers until dough is smooth and holds its shape. Wrap in plastic wrap and refrigerate 30 to 60 minutes.

When dough is ready, lay a sheet of plastic wrap on work surface. Place three-quarters of dough in center, reserving remainder for lattice top. Cover with another sheet of plastic wrap. Roll dough to 12-inch circle.

Coat pie plate with nonstick cooking spray. Remove top layer of plastic wrap. Carefully place rolled-out dough into prepared pie plate, pastry side down. Gently press dough into bottom and sides of pie plate. Discard remaining plastic.

TO PREPARE FILLING AND ASSEMBLE PIE
Preheat oven to 350°F. In medium mixing bowl, combine water, sugar, cherries, all-purpose flour, cinnamon, and soy flour. Spread filling in pie shell. Roll out remaining dough. Cut 1/2 inch wide strips. Crisscross strips over filling to form a lattice. Dust with turbinado sugar. Cover edges with a 2-inch strip of aluminum foil to prevent excessive browning. Bake 60 to 65 minutes or until golden brown.

Yield: 8 servings

Nutrition Per Serving
Calories: 358
Total fat: 12.6 g
Cholesterol: 11 mg
Carbohydrates: 60.2 g
Dietary fiber: 2.6 g
Protein: 5.4 g

Health Benefit: Cherries are a good source of potassium, and though lower in calcium than blueberries or blackberries, they contain a whopping 1,349 IU of vitamin A per one-cup serving. Cherries also contain 0.10 mg of vitamin B6, and 0.2 mg of zinc, and small amounts of thiamin, riboflavin, niacin, and folate.

GOLDEN PLUM COBBLER

Sweet, juicy, and fragrant with purple plums, this pie is for all seasons.

LARGE, TENDER LOWER-FAT PIECRUST
1 1/2 cups plus 2 tablespoons unbleached all-purpose flour
1/2 cup plus 2 tablespoons Soya powder
3 tablespoons granulated sugar
1/4 teaspoon salt
2 tablespoons cornstarch
4 tablespoons light butter
1/4 cup plus 2 tablespoons cooking oil
3 to 4 tablespoons ice water

FILLING
1 cup brown sugar, packed
1/2 cup papaya syrup
1/2 teaspoon cinnamon
dash of salt
1 teaspoon lemon zest
1 1/2 teaspoons lemon juice
2 cans (16 ounces each) purple plums
1/4 cup golden raisins
2 tablespoons cornstarch
1/4 cup unbleached flour
1 tablespoon soy flour

TO PREPARE PIECRUST
In medium mixing bowl, combine all-purpose flour, Soya powder, sugar, salt, and cornstarch.

In small saucepan, melt butter over low heat. Add cooking oil. Remove from heat. Carefully stir butter mixture into flour mixture with a fork. Mixture will be crumbly. Add ice water, 1 tablespoon at a time, adding just enough to make dough pliable and to bind the dough. Knead lightly with fingers until dough is smooth and holds its shape. Wrap dough in plastic wrap. Refrigerate 30 to 60 minutes.

When dough is ready, lay a sheet of plastic wrap on work surface, and place two-thirds of dough in center, reserving remainder for lattice top. Cover with another sheet of plastic wrap. Roll dough to 14 x 10-inch oblong.

Coat 13 x 9-inch baking dish with nonstick cooking spray. Remove top layer of plastic wrap. Carefully place rolled-out dough into the prepared dish, pastry side down. Gently press dough into bottom of dish and about 1/2 to 1 inch up the sides. Discard remaining plastic.

TO PREPARE FILLING AND ASSEMBLE PIE
Preheat oven to 350°F. Pit plums and discard seeds. In large bowl, combine sugar, papaya fruit syrup, cinnamon, salt, lemon zest, lemon juice, plums, raisins, cornstarch, all-purpose flour, and soy flour. Pour plum mixture into piecrust.

Roll out remaining pastry. Cut into ½ inch wide strips. Crisscross strips over the filling to form a lattice. With a knife, loosen lip of bottom pastry. Fold over lattice edges. Cover edges with a 2-inch strip of aluminum foil to prevent excessive browning.

Bake 60 to 65 minutes or until golden brown.

Yield: 12 servings

Nutrition Per Serving
Calories: 318
Total fat: 11.6 g
Cholesterol: 10 mg
Carbohydrates: 50.7 g
Dietary fiber: 1.8 g
Protein: 4.4 g

Health Benefit: Papaya syrup concentrate, which can be purchased in health-food stores, is high in potassium, as are plums.

BEST EVER PEACH COBBLER

This recipe comes from a gentleman who once served the best barbecue west of the Mississippi. The cobbler probably brought in as many customers as the barbecue. This version retains the sweet peachy flavor while cutting some fat from the crust.

PIECRUST
1 Large Tender Lower-fat Piecrust (see index)

FILLING
1 can (29 ounces) sliced peaches, including juice
1 3/4 cups water
1/2 cup granulated sugar
1/3 cup cornstarch
1 tablespoon soy flour

TO PREPARE PIECRUST
Prepare piecrust dough according to recipe instructions.

When ready to use, place two-thirds of dough in center of the plastic wrap, reserving remainder for lattice top. Cover with another sheet of plastic wrap. Roll dough to a 14 x 10-inch oblong.

Coat 13 x 9-inch baking dish with nonstick cooking spray. Remove top layer of plastic wrap. Carefully place rolled out dough into prepared dish, pasty side down. Gently press dough into bottom of dish and about 1/2 to 1 inch up sides. Discard remaining plastic.

TO PREPARE FILLING AND ASSEMBLE PIE

Preheat oven to 350°F. In large saucepan, combine peaches, including juice, water, sugar, cornstarch, and soy flour over low heat. Turn heat to medium, stirring the mixture constantly until it barely begins to boil. Remove from heat and pour mixture into piecrust.

Roll out remaining dough. Cut into strips ½ inch wide. Crisscross strips over filling to form a lattice. With a knife, loosen lip of bottom pastry. Fold over lattice edges. Cover edges with a 2-inch strip of aluminum foil to prevent excessive browning. Bake 60 to 65 minutes or until golden brown.

Yield: 12 servings

Nutrition Per Serving
Calories: 270
Total fat: 11.6 g
Cholesterol: 10 mg
Carbohydrates: 39.3 g
Dietary fiber: 1.9 g
Protein: 4 g

Health Benefit: A good choice for a pie filling, peaches are low in calories and rich in vitamin A, with one cup containing 691 IU of vitamin A plus 254 mg of potassium. Peaches contain no fat or sodium, and, of course, like all fruits, they have no cholesterol.

BANANA SPLIT PIE

Ice cream dripping with chocolate and bananas has long been an all-American treat.

PIECRUST
1 Tender Lower-fat Piecrust (see index), baked and cooled

FILLING
3 medium bananas
1 tablespoon lemon juice
1 pint fat-free or low-fat strawberry ice cream
1 package nonfat dessert topping mix
1 jar maraschino cherries, drained
1/4 cup chopped pecans (optional)

STRAWBERRY SAUCE
1 cup strawberries, sliced
3/4 cup granulated sugar
2 tablespoons cornstarch
1 cup plus 1 tablespoon water

TO PREPARE PIECRUST
Prepare piecrust dough according to recipe instructions. Bake and cool.

TO PREPARE FILLING
Thinly slice bananas over baked piecrust. Sprinkle with lemon juice. Soften ice cream. Spoon over bananas. Freeze until firm.

Prepare nonfat dessert topping mix. Spread over pie filling. Top with cherries. Sprinkle with pecans, if desired. Serve with strawberry sauce.

TO PREPARE STRAWBERRY SAUCE

In heavy saucepan, bring strawberries, sugar, cornstarch, and water to a boil over medium heat, stirring constantly. Reduce heat. Cook until mixture thickens. Continue stirring, simmering 5 to 6 minutes. Remove from heat.

Refrigerate until ready to serve.

Yield: 8 servings

Nutrition Per Serving

Calories: 341
Total fat: 11.5 g
Cholesterol: 20 mg
Carbohydrates: 78 g
Dietary fiber: 1 g
Protein: 3.7 g

Health Benefit: Strawberries contain 16 mg of magnesium, 0.19 mg of zinc, and 0.34 mg of niacin as well as small amounts of other minerals.

*Analysis based on low-fat ice cream

FRESH STRAWBERRY PIE

This recipe is an adaptation from a recipe of a dear lady and excellent cook, Mrs. Oliver Ridgon. It comes courtesy of her daughter-in-law, Carol Fisher.

PIECRUST
1 Tender Lower-fat Piecrust (see index)

FILLING
1 1/3 cups granulated sugar
1/4 cup cornstarch
1/2 cup water
1 tablespoon lemon juice
1/8 teaspoon salt
1 quart strawberries, washed, and thinly sliced
1 package nonfat dessert topping, optional

TO PREPARE PIECRUST
Prepare piecrust dough according to recipe instructions. Bake and cool.

TO PREPARE FILLING
In medium saucepan, combine sugar, cornstarch, water, lemon juice, and salt. Cook slowly over low heat, about 8 to 10 minutes or until mixture thickens and turns clear. Cool. Spoon strawberries into baked piecrust. Pour filling on top. Refrigerate 3 hours or until set. When ready to serve, top with prepared dessert topping, if desired. Refrigerate leftovers.

Yield: 8 servings

Nutrition Per Serving
Calories: 277
Total fat: 8.8 g
Cholesterol: 8 mg
Carbohydrates: 48 g
Dietary fiber: 3 g
Protein: 2.6 g.

Health Benefit: Strawberries are a good source of antioxidants. Per cup, raw strawberries contain 85 mg of vitamin C, 247 mg of potassium, and 0.57 mg of iron.

Ever Lovin'
Cookies

THE INCREDIBLE COOKIE

Nothing smells quite as good as homemade cookies fresh from the oven. And when delicious cookies are healthier and lower in calories than their higher-fat cookie cousins, they can add spice to your life every day of the year. Cookies are for all seasons--spring, summer, fall, winter--Christmas, Easter, Thanksgiving, Halloween, Valentine's Day, and, of course, birthdays.

To meet heart-healthy guidelines, shortening is never used in these cookies, or for that matter, in any recipe in this book. These cookies are made with oil or light butter. Tofu is often used as a partial fat substitute. All the recipes use soy in some form—either soy flour or tofu. **Use only low-fat silken tofu.**

These cookies, then, are for the health-conscious cooks who want wholesome, satisfying, lower-fat treats. The secret to baking lower-fat cookies is incredibly easy. Replace half or more of the fat in traditional recipes with tofu. The result--cookies that are higher in protein than cookies made merely with egg whites. Any reduction in saturated shortening or butter reduces cholesterol.

Many of the cookie recipes feature antioxidant rich dried fruits. Fruits naturally make cookies sweet and delicious.

To make fabulous cookies, follow these simple tips:

■ Assemble all ingredients before you begin.
■ Preheat oven for at least 20 minutes before baking.
■ Always use an oven thermometer.

■ Use standard measuring spoons and measuring cups. Measure all ingredients carefully, leveling off top of dry ingredients with a knife blade.

■ Measure and then sift flour, especially soy flour if it is lumpy.

■ Always sift baking soda and baking powder to prevent lumps.

■ Do not use fat-free margarine as a substitute for light butter since fat-free margarine products are watery and change the texture of baked goods.

■ Use heavy aluminum baking sheets. The heavier the baking sheet, the more evenly the heat will be distributed. Insulated cookie sheets cause cookies to brown less on the bottom. Cookies will take slightly longer to bake.

■ Cool baking sheets before adding a second batch of cookie dough.

■ Coat baking sheets with nonstick cooking spray.

■ Never overbake cookies. Even one minute can make a big difference. Check cookies at the minimum baking time. Continue checking every minute until done. Most cookies will barely be brown on the edge. Remove from oven when firmly set.

■ Cool cookies on cookie sheet before transferring to a wire rack. Do not stack cookies while they are hot. They need air to circulate. Stacked hot cookies may stick together or become soggy.

■ When rolling out dough, add only small amounts of flour. Fit a floured pastry cloth over the rolling pin. Too much flour makes tough cookies.

■ Store soft cookies in a container with a tight-fitting lid. Place sheets of waxed paper between layers so cookies won't stick together. Frosted or filled cookies should be stored in a single layer.

■ Store crisp cookies in a container with a loose-fitting cover. Do not leave tofu cookies in excessive heat or humidity. Any fresh products will spoil under moist conditions.

OATMEAL COOKIES

These cookies are excellent anytime of the year. Since they contain healthy oats and soy's goodness, you'll want to serve them often.

3/4 cup light butter
1/4 cup cooking oil
1 cup brown sugar, firmly packed
1/2 cup granulated sugar
4 egg whites
1/4 cup low-fat silken tofu, drained and mashed
1 1/2 teaspoons vanilla
2 cups all-purpose flour
1 teaspoon baking soda
3/4 teaspoon allspice
1/2 teaspoon salt
3 cups oats, uncooked
3/4 cup raisins
1/4 cup walnuts, optional
1 teaspoon cinnamon, if desired

In large mixing bowl, cream butter and sugars. Add egg, egg whites, tofu, and vanilla.

In separate bowl, combine flour, baking soda, allspice, and salt. Stir into wet ingredients. Mix well. Stir in oats, raisins, walnuts, and cinnamon.

Preheat oven to 350°F. Coat cookie sheets with nonstick cooking spray. Drop dough by rounded teaspoonfuls. Bake 8-10 minutes or until cookies are barely brown on edges. Cool 3-5 minutes. Remove to wire racks.

Yield: 70 cookies

Nutrition Per Serving
Calories: 85
Total fat: 3.2 g
Cholesterol: 5 mg.
Carbohydrates: 12.9 mg.
Dietary fiber: 1.1 g
Protein: 1.6 g

Health Benefit:
Oats and soy products
can now be listed on
food labeling packages
as cholesterol lowering
foods. Add these to
your diet often.

Variation: Cookies from a mix: You can make cookies from a prepacked mix. For Oatmeal Chocolate Chip cookies, simply use the 1 lb.1.5 oz package of Chocolate Chip Cookie Mix. Add the usual amount of butter or oil as recommended by the package recipe. Add eggs as recommended via package instructions. Stir in 1/4 cup silken tofu (drained and mashed) and 1/4 cup all-purpose flour. Bake according to package directions. You can use whole-grain cookie mixes the same way. Simply add the extra tofu and additional flour to make dough slightly stiff. Otherwise, follow package instructions.

SNICKERDOODLES

An old American classic, these spicy cookies are delicious with herbal tea, hot chocolate, or by themselves.

2 cups granulated sugar
1/4 cup plus 1 tablespoon cooking oil
1/4 cup plus 1 teaspoon baby food prunes
1 1/2 teaspoons vanilla extract
1/2 cup tofu, drained and mashed
2 3/4 cups unbleached all-purpose flour
1 tablespoon soy flour
1 1/4 teaspoons cream of tartar
1/2 teaspoon baking soda
1/4 teaspoon salt
4 tablespoons granulated sugar
4 teaspoons cinnamon

In large bowl, combine 2 cups sugar, oil, baby food prunes, vanilla, and tofu. Beat until creamy. In separate bowl, combine all-purpose flour, soy flour, cream of tartar, baking soda, and salt. Stir in wet ingredients. With hands, work dough until it binds together. Shape into 1-inch balls. In small bowl, combine 4 tablespoons sugar and cinnamon.

Preheat oven to 350°F. Coat a cookie sheet with nonstick cooking spray. Roll dough balls in sugar-cinnamon mixture. Place 2-inches apart on prepared cookie sheet. Flatten tops slightly with a glass. Bake 10 to 12 minutes or until barely set. Cool 3 to 5 minutes. Remove to wire racks.

Yield: 3 dozen cookies

Nutrition Per Serving
Calories: 103
Total fat: 2.1 g
Cholesterol: 0
Carbohydrates: 20.2 g
Dietary fiber: 0.8 g
Protein: 1.4 g

Health Benefit: Complex grains make these low-fat cookies richer in fiber.

PEANUT BUTTER COOKIES

Peanut butter cookies have long been a winner in American cookie jars. Keep up the tradition with these lower-fat treats.

1/4 cup cooking oil
3/4 cup reduced-fat peanut butter
1/4 cup maple syrup
1 1/4 cups brown sugar, packed
1/2 cup tofu, drained and mashed
1 teaspoon vanilla extract
1 cup unbleached all-purpose flour
1/4 cup whole-wheat flour
1 teaspoon baking soda
1/4 teaspoon salt
3 tablespoons wheat germ

In large bowl, combine oil, peanut butter, maple syrup, brown sugar, tofu, and vanilla. Beat until creamy.

In separate bowl, combine all-purpose flour, whole-wheat flour, baking soda, salt, and wheat germ. Stir in wet ingredients. Mix well.

Preheat oven to 350°F. Coat cookie sheet with nonstick cooking spray. Drop dough by rounded teaspoonfuls. Bake 6-8 minutes or just until cookies are set. Cool 3 to 5 minutes Remove to wire racks.

Yield: 4 dozen cookies

Nutrition Per Serving
Calories: 71
Total fat: 2.5 g
Cholesterol: 0
Carbohydrates: 10 g
Dietary fiber: 0.5 g
Protein: 1 g

Health Benefit: Peanut butter, like tofu and wheat germ, is an excellent source of protein.

GINGERBREAD COOKIES

These spicy cookies have long pleased children of all ages, especially when cut into shapes and decorated for Christmas or other occasions.

1 1/4 cups brown sugar, packed
1/4 cup cooking oil
1/4 cup baby food prunes
1/3 cup cane syrup
1 egg white
3 tablespoons soy flour
3 1/4 cups unbleached all-purpose flour
1 teaspoon baking soda
1/4 teaspoon cream of tartar
1 teaspoon cinnamon
1/4 teaspoon ginger
1/8 teaspoon salt
1/4 teaspoon cloves
1/4 teaspoon allspice

In large bowl, combine brown sugar, cooking oil, baby food prunes, cane syrup, and egg white. Beat well. In a separate bowl, combine soy flour, all-purpose flour, baking soda, cream of tartar, cinnamon, ginger, salt, cloves, and allspice. Stir into wet ingredients. Mix well. When dough becomes too stiff for the mixer, stir by hand until well mixed. Cover dough with plastic wrap or put in an airtight storage container. Refrigerate 1 to 3 hours or overnight.

On a well-floured surface, roll out one-quarter to one-half dough at a time to 1/8-inch thickness. If dough is sticky, knead in the barest amount of flour to make it manageable.

Preheat oven to 325°F. Coat cookie sheets with nonstick cooking spray. Cut dough into shapes with large cookie cutters dusted with flour. Place cookies 1 inch apart on prepared cookie sheets.

Repeat process with remaining dough. Bake 7 to 8 minutes or until set. Cool 3 to 5 minutes. Remove to wire racks.

Yield: 2 dozen large cookies

Nutrition Per Serving
Calories: 141
Total fat 2.4 g
Cholesterol: 0
Carbohydrates: 28 g
Dietary fiber: 0.7 g
Protein: 2 g

Health Benefit: Soy flour adds moistness, allowing a significant reduction of shortening. Since shortening contains 1,812 calories and 205 g of fat per cup, the saving is a heart-healthy choice.

Decorating Tips: Use candy red-hots for eyes and buttons. For gingerbread boys, pipe white icing in strings around the legs and arms; for gingerbread girls, pipe thicker layers of icing. Pipe collar and hair. For Halloween, cut into pumpkin shapes. Ice with orange icing. Decorate tops with candy corn.

RICH DEVIL'S FOOD COOKIES

If you love chocolate, these moist and delicious cookies, with a rich brownie taste, will satisfy your biggest chocolate craving– with little fat.

COOKIES
1 1/2 cups unbleached all-purpose flour
1/2 cup cocoa
1/2 teaspoon baking soda
1 teaspoon baking powder
1/4 teaspoon salt
3 tablespoons cooking oil
1 ounce unsweetened chocolate
1 1/4 cups light-brown sugar, packed
1/4 cup tofu, drained and mashed
3 egg whites
2 tablespoons light corn syrup
1 teaspoon vanilla

GLAZE
1 cup confectioners sugar
2 tablespoons cocoa
6 teaspoons water
1/2 teaspoon vanilla

In medium bowl, combine flour, cocoa, baking soda, baking powder, and salt. In small glass bowl, combine oil and chocolate; microwave 1 minute on high. Stir until smooth.

In separate bowl, beat brown sugar, tofu, and egg whites 3 to 5 minutes. Slowly stir in melted chocolate mixture, corn syrup, and vanilla, beating 1 minute to blend. Stir into dry ingredients.

Preheat oven to 350°F. Coat baking sheet with nonstick cooking spray. Drop dough by rounded teaspoonfuls, leaving 2 inches between cookies. Bake 7 to 9 minutes or just until the centers begin to set. Cool 3 to 5 minutes. Remove to wire racks. Spoon glaze on top.

TO MAKE THE GLAZE

Mix together confectioners sugar, cocoa, water, and vanilla, stirring until smooth. Spoon 1 teaspoon over each cookie.

Yield: 32 cookies

Nutrition Per Serving
Calories: 78
Total fat: 2.1 g
Cholesterol: 0
Carbohydrates: 14.4 g
Dietary fiber: 0.8 g
Protein: 1.5 g

Health Benefit: Tofu makes this heart-healthy recipe cholesterol free. Many health experts agree that a tofu-based diet could drastically lower cholesterol and save lives. Research suggests that the lecithin and linoleic acid in tofu may have the ability to assist the body in lowering cholesterol levels by helping to break down cholesterol and fat deposits. Tofu also contains B vitamins, which many health authorities suggest aids in lowering heart attack risk.

MOM'S SUGAR COOKIES

Bring in the kids and grandkids and have some real old-fashioned fun baking and decorating cookies. These cookies are delicious.

1 1/2 cups sifted confectioners' sugar
1 cup light butter
1 egg
1/4 cup low-fat silken tofu, drained and mashed
1 1/2 teaspoons vanilla
3 cups all-purpose flour
1 teaspoon baking soda
1 teaspoon cream of tartar

In large bowl, cream sugar and butter. Mix in egg, tofu, and vanilla. Mix well.

In separate bowl, mix flour, soda, and cream of tartar. Stir into wet ingredients. Mix well.

Cover dough with plastic wrap. Refrigerate 3-4 hours.

On well-floured surface, roll one-fourth dough to 3/16-inch thickness. Cut out shapes with cookie cutters. Decorate as desired. Repeat process with remaining dough.

Preheat oven to 350°F. Coat cookie sheets with nonstick cooking spray. Place cookies 1-inch apart. Bake 7-8 minutes or just until cookies are set. Cool 3 to 5 minutes. Remove to wire racks.

Yield: 5 dozen

Nutrition Per Serving
Calories: 73.4
Total Fat: 4.7 g
Cholesterol: 8 mg
Carbohydrates: 7.5 g
Dietary fiber: 0.2 g
Protein: 1.0 g

Health Benefit:
Tofu increases the nutritive value of an otherwise lower nutrition cookie. Adding even small amounts of tofu increases calcium and B vitamins.

Decorating tip: *For Christmas, one of my favorite cutouts is the rocking horse. Use candy for the eyes. When cookies have cooled, use a cake decorating tube and pipe icing around neck and along bottom of the rocker.*

Variation: Sugar Cookies from a mix: *You can make cookies from a prepacked mix. Simply use the 1 lb.1.5 oz package of Sugar Cookie Mix. Add the usual amount of butter as recommended by the package recipe. Add eggs as recommended via package instructions. Stir in 1/4 cup silken tofu (drained and mashed) and 1/4 cup all-purpose flour. Bake according to package directions. If dough is too soft, work in additional all-purpose flour.*

LEBKUCHEN

Naturally low in fat, these cookies are delicious.

COOKIES
1/2 cup brown-rice syrup
1/2 cup cane syrup
1 1/2 cups brown sugar, packed
1 tablespoon grated lemon peel
2 egg whites
2 tablespoons soy flour
2 1/4 cups plus 2 tablespoons unbleached all-purpose flour
1/2 teaspoon baking soda
1/4 teaspoon salt
3/4 teaspoon cinnamon
3/4 teaspoon ginger
3/4 teaspoon cloves
1/4 teaspoon allspice
1/4 cup diced dried apricots
1/4 cup candied orange peel
1/3 cup chopped almonds (optional)
Sliced almonds (optional)

GLAZE
1/2 cup confectioners sugar
2 to 4 tablespoons water

Heat rice syrup and cane syrup in a medium saucepan over medium heat. Heat mixture barely to a bubble stage. Do not boil. Remove from heat. Let cool. Add brown sugar, lemon peel, and egg whites.

In medium bowl, combine soy flour, all-purpose flour, baking soda, salt, cinnamon, ginger, cloves, allspice, apricots, orange peel, and chopped almonds. Add syrup mixture and stir well. For easier handling, cover with plastic wrap and refrigerate 1 to 2 hours or overnight.

In small bowl, combine confectioners sugar and water for the glaze. The glaze should be thin. Set aside.

Preheat oven to 400°F. Coat cookie sheets with nonstick cooking spray. Shape dough into 1-inch balls. Place 2 inches apart on prepared cookie sheets. Gently press to 1/4-inch thickness. Press 1 almond slice in center of each cookie.

Bake 5 to 9 minutes or until set. Immediately remove cookies to wire racks. Brush with glaze. Cool completely.

Yield: 5 dozen cookies

Nutrition Per Serving
Calories: 60
Total fat: 0
Cholesterol 0
Carbohydrates: 14 g
Dietary fiber: 0.3 g
Protein: 0.8 g

Health Benefit: These cookies are cholesterol-free, fat-free, and dairy-free. As a bonus, cinnamon contains per tablespoon 3.7 g of dietary fiber, 34 g of potassium, 84 g of calcium, 2.6 mg of iron, 18 IU of vitamin A, and slight traces of B vitamins.

Tip: *Gluten-free brown rice syrup, thick like honey and sweet as the finest syrup, can be used on pancakes, biscuits, or toast.*

MINI CANDY BIT COOKIES

Dotted with bits of candy, these cookies offer kids a double treat.

3 tablespoons baby food prunes
1/2 cup light butter
3/4 cup granulated sugar
1/4 cup brown sugar, packed
2 egg whites
1 teaspoon vanilla extract
1 1/2 cups unbleached all-purpose flour
1/4 cup soy flour
1 teaspoon baking soda
3/4 teaspoon salt
1/2 cup mini candy chips

In medium bowl, combine baby food prunes, butter, granulated sugar, and brown sugar until creamy. Add egg whites and vanilla. Continue beating until well blended.

In separate bowl, combine all-purpose flour, soy flour, baking soda, and salt. Stir in wet ingredients. Mix well. Add candy chips.

Preheat oven to 375°F. Coat cookie sheets with nonstick cooking spray. Drop dough by rounded teaspoonfuls. Bake 8 to 9 minutes or just until cookies are set. Cool 5 to 10 minutes. Remove to wire racks.

Yield: 3 dozen cookies

Nutrition Per Serving
Calories: 71
Total fat: 2.2 g
Cholesterol: 7 mg
Carbohydrates: 12 g
Dietary fiber: 0.5 g
Protein: 1 g

Health Benefit: Soy flour packs in potassium, fiber, calcium, B vitamins, and vitamin E.

APPENDIX

More About Soy

The Top Ten Benefits of Soy

1. **Antioxidant.** Soyfoods contain antioxidant-compounds which protect cells from damage caused by unstable oxygen molecules called *free radicals*. Free radicals are believed to be responsible for initiating many forms of cancer, as well as premature aging. In addition, the oxidation of LDL, or "bad cholesterol", is believed to promote the formation of plaque.

2. **Breast Cancer.** A major study in Singapore revealed that women who eat soyfoods are at lower risk of developing breast cancer than those who don't. Asian women, who typically eat a soy-based diet, have much lower levels of breast cancer than do their Western counterparts. Test tube studies, as well as those involving laboratory animals, have shown evidence that compounds in soy can inhibit the growth of breast cancer cells.

3. **Cholesterol Lowering.** Scores of studies from around the world attest to soy's cholesterol-lowering properties, especially for people with high cholesterol levels.

4. **Colon Cancer.** A recent U.S. study showed that Americans who made soybeans and tofu a regular part of their diet had significantly lower rates of colon cancer than those who didn't eat soy.

5. **Hip Fractures.** Hip fractures owing to osteoporosis are a major problem among elderly women in the United States. Japanese women have half the rate of hip fractures as American women; preliminary studies suggest that soy may help retain bone mass.

6. **Hot Flashes.** Half of all menopausal women in the U. S. complain of hot flashes, a problem that is so rare in Japan that there's not even a word for it. Some researchers believe that special compounds in soy, called phytoestrogens, may help the Japanese women to stay cooler.

7. **Immunity.** Studies show that soybean peptides (chains of amino acids) can boost the immune system, helping the body to fight disease.

8. **Kidney Disease.** Soy protein is easier on the kidneys, the main filtering organ of the body, than is animal protein and may slow down or prevent kidney damage in people with impaired kidney function.

9. **Lung Cancer.** Studies have linked soy consumption to lower rates of lung cancer.

10. **Prostate cancer.** A major study of Japanese men in Hawaii found a direct correlation between consumption of tofu and lower rates of prostate cancer. Studies of soy compounds have shown that they can inhibit the growth of prostate cancer cells in laboratory cultures.

SOYFOODS MAY HAVE BENEFICIAL EFFECT ON BREAST CANCER

Soybeans - and the foods made from them - have a unique make-up. They are rich in a group of compounds called isoflavones, which may have some intriguing effects on health.

Isoflavones are one type of a larger group of chemicals called phytochemicals (plant chemicals). These are a group of diverse chemicals with a wide range of effects on health, and they are found only in plant foods (grains, beans, fruits, vegetables, nuts and seeds).

Isoflavones are also sometimes called phytoestrogens, which translates to "plant estrogens." They have some properties that are similar to human estrogen, but their effects are much weaker. These isoflavones may have some beneficial effects on breast cancer, which is the second most common cause of death among American women and is the leading cause of death in women between the ages of 35 and 44.

Breast cancer is a complex disease and scientists don't yet understand exactly what causes it, but they do know that lifestyle affects risk. For example, both alcohol and smoking raise the risk for breast cancer. Certain dietary changes may lower that risk.

Breast cancer rates vary dramatically among different groups of women. American women are four times more likely to die of breast cancer than Japanese women. Although there are a number of possible reasons for this difference, one reason may be that Japanese women consume soyfoods. Some research shows that women who eat soy have less breast cancer than those who don't. As little as one serving of soyfoods a day (1/2 cup tofu or 1 cup soy milk) may be enough to reduce risk.

Breast cancer is an "estrogen dependent" cancer. When estrogen attaches to sites on the breast tissue, it can induce the cancer process. Isoflavones look like estrogen, so they can attach to the same sites on breast tissue. By occupying these sites, they may keep the more powerful estrogen from exerting its cancer-causing effects. One interesting suggestion is that soy isoflavones act in a way similar to the drug tamoxifen, which is widely used to treat breast cancer. Researchers need to gather much more data before they can say with any certainty that soy will lower breast cancer risk. But for now, it looks like adding some soyfoods to the diet might be a good idea for all women.

SOME MORE SOYFOODS

When it comes to a versatile food, it is hard to beat the soybean. Soybeans not only offer great health benefits, but they are easy to add to your diet, and they taste good. You are probably already eating more soy-based foods than you realize. When you read the label on some of your favorite prepared foods, you may notice that some type of soy product is listed on the label, such as lecithin, textured soy protein, soy protein concentrates and soy oil. Over 75 percent of vegetable oils and fats on the market today are soybean oil. Soybeans are popular in food manufacturing because of their versatility.

Here are a few more of the most common soyfoods on the market today. Some of these foods may be familiar, and others may be new. All of them are worth trying.

Edamame: Also known as "Sweet Beans," edamame comes from large soybeans harvested when the beans are still green. These sweet tasting beans can be served as a snack or a main vegetable dish. They are high in protein and fiber and contain no cholesterol. Edamame often is found in Asian and natural food stores.

Isolated Soy Proteins: When soybeans are processed, the hulls and oil are removed, leaving "defatted flakes." Soy flakes are used for defatted soy flour, soy concentrates, and soy isolates. When protein is removed from defatted flakes, the result is soy protein isolates, the most highly refined soy protein. Containing 92 percent protein, soy protein isolates possess the greatest amount of protein of all soy products. They are a highly digestible source of amino acids (building blocks of protein necessary for human growth and maintenance).

Lecithins: Extracted from soybean oil, lecithin is used in food manufacturing as an emulsifier in products high in fats and oils. They also promote stabilization, antioxidation, crystallization and spattering control. Powdered lecithins can be found in natural and health food stores.

Natto: Natto is made of fermented, cooked whole soybeans. Because the fermentation process breaks down the beans' complex proteins, natto is more easily digested than whole soybeans. It has a sticky, viscous coating with a cheesy texture. In Asian countries, natto traditionally is served as a topping for rice, in miso soups, and is used with vegetables. Natto can be found in Asian and natural food stores.

U.S. SOYFOODS DIRECTORY

Isoflavone Concentration in Soyfoods

Isoflavones are found in soyfoods both with and without a sugar molecule attached. The two primary isoflavones in soybeans are daidzein and genistein and their respective glucosides, genistin and daidzin. Soyfoods typically contain more genistein than daidzein, although this ratio varies among different soy products.

On a dry weight basis, raw soybeans contain between two and four milligrams of total isoflavones/gram. Soyfoods differ somewhat in their concentration of isoflavones, but all of the traditional soyfoods, such as tofu, soy milk, tempeh, and miso, are rich sources of isoflavones, providing about 30 to 40 milligrams per serving. One-half cup of soy flour contains approximately 50 milligrams of isoflavone. Only two soy products, soy sauce and soy oil, do not contain isoflavones.

Soy protein concentrates (65% soy protein), a widely used ingredient (frequently used in soy burgers), may or may not contain nutritionally significant amounts of isoflavones depending on how the product was processed. Both soy flour and textured soy protein are rich in isoflavones. Soy protein isolate (90% soy protein) contains less than these products but still has significant amounts.

A group of soyfoods, often referred to as second generation products (such as soy hot dogs and soy-based ice cream) can have much lower amounts of isoflavones because they frequently contain considerable amounts of non-soy ingredients.

Estimated Values for Isoflavone Content of Selected Soyfoods*

(This information was distributed as part of a presentation at the American Dietetic Association 80th Annual Meeting and Exhibition, held October 27-30, 1997, in Boston, Massachusetts, by James W. Anderson, M.D. Professor of Medicine andClinical Nutrition University of Kentucky, Lexington, KY. Phone 606-281-4954; fax 606-233-3832. e-mail: jwandersmd@aol.com.

Food	Svg. Size g	Serving Size Measure	Protein g/100g	Genistein ng/g prot.	Total Isoflavone ug/g prot	Isoflavone mg/g prot	mg/sv g
Mature soybeans, uncooked	93	1/2 cup	37.0	1106	1891	5.1	175.06
Roasted soybeans	86	1/2 cup	35.2	1214	1942	5.5	167.0
Soy flour	21	1/4 cup	37.8	1185	2084	5.5	43.8
Textured soy protein, dry	30	1/4 cup	18.0	472	928	5.2	27.8
Green soygeans, uncooked	128	1/2 cup	16.6	301	548	3.3	70.1
Soy milk	228	1 cup	4.4	30	56	2.0	20.0
Tempeh, uncooked	114	4 oz.	17.0	277	531	3.1	60.5
Tofu, uncooked	114	4 oz.	15.8	209	336	2.1	38.3
Soy isolate, dry	28	1 oz.	92.0	1100	2174	2.2	56.5
Soy concentrate, dry	28	1 oz.	63.6	111	195	0.3	12.4

* These values were obtained from the published literature and from analyses we have obtained for selected products.

The isoflavone content varies widely among soybean varieties and from product to product based on manufacturing process and source of soy protein. These estimates are our best calculation of isoflavone values provided by currently available products. The references listed below provide more detailed information about the different isoflavones in specific products.

References

1. Coward L, Barnes NC, Setchell KDR, Barnes S. Journal of Agricultural and Food Chemistry 1993; 41: 1961-67.
2. Dwyer JT, Goldin BR, Saul N, Gualtieri L, Barakat S, Adlercreutz H. Journal of the American Dietetic Association 1994; 94: 739-43.
3. Franke AA, Custer LJ, Cerna CM, Narala KK. Journal of Agricultural and Food Chemistry 1994; 42: 1905-13.
4. Reinli K, Block G. Nutrition and Cancer 1996; 26: 123-48.
5. Wang H, Murphy PA. Journal of Agricultural and Food Chemistry 1994; 1666-1673.

Questions may be directed to:

Dr. James Anderson, B402 VA Medical Center I I IC, 2250 Leestown Rd., Lexington, NY 40511

Iron in Soyfoods

Soybeans and the foods made from them are high in iron. However, soy is also high in two components that interfere with iron absorption. First, soyfoods are high in phytates. Even very small amounts of phytate in a food can greatly reduce the amount of iron absorbed from that food or from other foods eaten at the same meal. The type of protein in soyfoods also reduces iron absorption.

Their high phytate and protein content means that iron is not well absorbed from soyfoods. But soy is very high in iron which partly makes up for poorer absorption. Also, adding soy protein to meat mixtures like hamburger does not raise risk for anemia. This is because soy is not only high in iron, but can actually increase the iron absorbed from meat.

Even though all soyfoods - like tofu, soy milk and tempeh - contain soy protein and phytates, the amount of iron absorbed from these different foods varies quite a bit. For example, iron absorption from fermented soyfoods like tempeh is quite good. Absorption is also better from softer tofu (like silken tofu) than from firm tofu.

In addition, vitamin C can increase absorption of iron from soyfoods and other plant foods when consumed at the same time. The amount of vitamin C in just 1/2 cup of orange juice can double iron absorption. Many plant foods are also rich in vitamin C, which enhances iron absorption. For these two reasons, it is relatively easy to meet iron needs with these foods.

Iron Content of Soyfoods

Miso (2 Tablespoons) 0.95mg
Soybeans (1/2 cup) 4.42mg
Soy flour (1/4 cup) 1.20mg
Soy milk (1 cup) 1.38mg
Roasted soynuts (1/2 cup) 3.40mg
Tempeh (1/2 cup) 1.88mg
Tofu (1/2 cup) 6.60mg

Note: The recommended dietary allowance for iron is 10-15 milligrams for adults.

Ideas for Adding Vitamin C to Meals
to Boost Iron Absorption

Cereal with soy milk...add sliced strawberries

Soy milk shake with banana...add orange juice

Stir-fried rice with tofu...add broccoli

Textured vegetable protein...add spaghetti sauce

Miso Soup with tofu chunks...add sliced cabbage

TOFU FOR EVERYONE

Tofu is the most popular soyfood... and with good reason! There are more than just a few different kinds of tofu on the market today, and the ways you can use it are limited only by your imagination. So, if your experience with tofu in the past was not so good, or if you limit yourself to only one or two kinds or uses of tofu, read on.

There are so many different tofus on the market that it is impossible to give a complete run-down on the nutrition in this newsletter. However, you can get detailed nutritional information on at least 18 different kinds of tofu at the USDA Nutrient Database for Standard Reference http:/www.nal.usda.gov/fnic/cgi-bin/nut_search.pl. You should know, though, that calories, fat, protein and carbohydrates will vary by manufacturer. Overall, tofu is a nutrient-rich, protein food and a good source of isoflavones, a phytochemical with many health benefits. Three ounces of tofu, which is considered a single serving (about the size of a deck of cards), contains approximately 30 mg of isoflavones, although this, too, will vary by manufacturer.

I often hear people say they avoid tofu because it contains a lot of fat. But as a dietitian I can say one thing: TOFU IS NOT HIGH FAT!! Even if the tofu you select has 9 grams of fat in a 3-ounce serving, that still is considered reasonable in a daily dietary plan. And of the 12 different kinds of tofu I found in a natural foods store this week, only one had 9 grams of fat. Most show 3, 5 or 6 grams of fat in a 3-ounce serving. This is comparable to the fat contained in fish, poultry, and lean cuts of beef and pork.

Compared to meat, poultry and fish, tofu may have slightly less protein, but this is not a problem for most of us who get plenty of protein in our diets. Tofu may be a good source of iron, averaging between 4% and 10% of our daily nutritional requirements. And tofu can be a good source of calcium, as well. Tofu is only a decent source of calcium if it is processed with a considerable amount of a calcium coagulant. The ones with the most calcium will show at least 10% of the minimum daily requirements in the Nutrition Facts label, which is pretty good as most foods go.

Using and Storing Different Types of Tofu

Silken tofu is probably the most common for many people as a result of shelf-stable packaging, which does not require refrigeration. Once opened though, it must be used within two days. This tofu is made differently than others and has a creamy, smooth texture. Never freeze silken tofu; it will ruin the texture. Available in soft, firm and extra firm 12-ounce packages, silken tofu works well for many dishes. Soft works well for salad dressings and dips, while firm and extra firm work well in stir fry dishes and baking.

Water-packed tofu also is very common. Usually sold in 1 pound blocks, this tofu is covered with water and wrapped in a plastic container. This tofu must always be refrigerated and covered with water, which should be changed daily. It should last a week or so in a refrigerator. Available in soft, firm, extra firm and regular, these tofus work great for everything. You can slice them, dice them, bake, grill, or barbecue them. You can even blend them up just like the silken tofu. Water packed tofu works best for freezing and then thawing, which makes the texture meatier, so that it tears, shreds, or crumbles more like meat.

Baked tofus are made with flavorings, like soy sauce, spices and herbs, and can be considered a true convenience soyfood... you just eat it hot or cold out of the package! No preparation is needed, unlike all the other tofu, although it still needs to be refrigerated. Cubed or sliced, baked tofu can be added to just about any dish. It can even be substituted for luncheon meat in sandwiches!

Smoked tofu is another one of the more convenient tofus! Smoked with added ingredients like sweeteners, spices, flavorings and herbs, it can easily be added to stir fry meals, salads, or sandwiches. Create instant meals by adding to pasta or rice. Varieties include savory, original, and hot & spicy. Smoked tofu needs to be refrigerated.

Eight Easy Ways to Use Tofu

1. Slice baked tofu and stuff in a pita pocket along with tomatoes and lettuce.

2. Cube smoked flavored tofu and stir into left over rice or noodles for a quick meal.

3. Cube flavored tofus over any green lettuce salad and turn it into a full meal.

4. Add cubed tofu to purchased meal starter frozen vegetables (1-ounce bags in the freezer case). These usually say add chicken, beef or pork, but tofu works and tastes great in these, especially the teriyaki and oriental varieties.

5. Whenever you make any stir fry dish, like beef and broccoli, or cashew chicken, throw in some chunks of tofu also.

6. Add cubes of tofu to meatless chili, soups, and stews.

7. Add crumbled tofu to cans of soup to boost protein and nutritional value.

SOY HELPS RELIEVE HOT FLUSHES

Adding soy protein to the diet may be a safe and effective way to combat hot flushes in postmenopausal women, according to Italian researchers in a recently published Reuters article. Dr. Paola Albertazzi of the University of Bologna and colleagues in Ferrara, Italy, report in the January issue of Obstetrics and Gynecology that soy was "...significantly superior to placebo in reducing the mean number of hot flushes per 24 hours after 4, 8, and 12 weeks of treatment." By the end of the study period, women taking soy had a 45% reduction in the number of hot flushes they experienced daily compared with a 30% reduction achieved in placebo-treated women. Similar findings from uncontrolled trials have been reported previously.

The article can be found on the Internet at Yahoo's Web site

\http://www.yahoo.com/headlines/980108/health/stories/soy

MORE CONSUMERS ARE TRYING SOY PRODUCTS

Soybean product trial usage is reaching relatively high levels among nutrition-conscious consumers, according to the 1997 National Report on Consumer Attitudes About Nutrition, published by the United Soybean Board (USB). Consumer perceptions stated in the report include:

■ Approximately 70% of consumers are very concerned with nutritional content and indicated they have tried some type of soy product.

■ 59% of Americans acknowledge that soy is healthy.

■ The perception of healthfulness is a primary driver of soy product trial and use. Among consumers who have tried soy products, 68% indicated soy is healthy.

■ Among consumers who indicate usage of soy products, tofu and soy burgers are the products most frequently incorporated into their diets.

A copy of the report can be obtained by calling the United Soybean Board at 1-800-TALKSOY.

Soyfoods USA Vol. 2 No. 3   April 16, 1997

NEW GENISTEIN RESEARCH

A component of soybeans called genistein so far looks extremely promising in preventing cancer, according to a report from the University of North Carolina at Chapel Hill. Researchers there have launched a new study of the protein, which stops human tumor cells from growing in laboratory culture and inhibits cancer in rats, to investigate the possibilities.

"We know the Japanese, who eat diets rich in soybeans, take in about 80 milligrams of genistein a day, and that's as much as 80 times more than we Americans do," said Steven Zeisel, chairman of nutrition at the UNC schools of public health and medicine. "Japanese people eat much of their genistein in the form of soybean curd they call tofu, and they have very low rates of breast and prostate cancer compared to us."

Because no scientific data exists yet on what genistein does in humans, the National Cancer Institute has asked the UNC researchers to look into it and is providing purified genistein as well as assisting in the study design. The institute is supporting their work with $785,000 for the first year and may expand the studies later.

"The institute has asked us to do two things," Zeisel said. "First, we will study healthy people and patients with prostate cancer to determine how high a dose people can take without having side effects. Once we establish that, we have an understanding that NCI will fund a larger study in which patients newly diagnosed with prostate cancer are randomly assigned either to receive nothing or receive medium to high doses of the protein."

Several weeks later, when patients go into surgery, researchers will compare their tumors to see whether treatment with genistein has affected tumor growth. "We expect that the protein should be able to convert cancer cells in a way that makes them less able to divide and grow," said Zeisel of the UNC Lineberger Comprehensive Cancer Center.

If the research turns out as hoped, it will provide the first evidence genistein can stop or retard cancer in humans, he said. The institute then will fund a large study of its effectiveness at multiple medical centers across the country.

The UNC work will begin in the metabolic kitchen, where research dietitian Marge Busby, along with other researchers will dole out a powdered form genistein to volunteers, gradually increasing the amount they consume. But Busby prefers to get her proteins in a more natural form.

"There are some great ways to enjoy soy," she said. "In fact, at my home we eat a lot of soy." One of her favorites is roasted soybeans, even though she knows they are a little high in fat. "But they are wonderful," she confesses. "I mix them up in coconut and raisins and dried apples and make my own little trail mix."

Busby's father prefers tempeh. "My dad is 74 years old, and he eats barbecued tempeh because he thinks it tastes great," she said. Her recipes are so good that she's gotten even her teenagers to eat tofu.

FDA PROPOSES HEALTH CLAIM FOR SOY PROTEIN

The Food and Drug Administration (FDA) has proposed allowing health claims about the role soy protein may have in reducing the risk of coronary heart disease (CHD) on the labels and labeling of foods containing soy protein. This proposal is based on the agency's determination that soy protein, as part of a diet low in saturated fat and cholesterol, may reduce the risk of CHD.

CHD is the most common, most frequently reported, and most serious form of cardiovascular disease, and is the number one cause of death in the United States. Despite the decline in deaths from CHD over the past 30 years, this disease still causes more than 500,000 deaths annually and contributes to another 250,000 deaths. High blood total cholesterol and high low-density lipoprotein (LDL) cholesterol levels are proven risk factors for CHD.

In proposing this health claim, the FDA concluded that foods containing protein from the soybean as part of a diet low in saturated fat and cholesterol may reduce the risk of heart disease by lowering blood total cholesterol and LDL-cholesterol. The amino acid content in soy protein is dfferent from animal and most other vegetable proteins and appears to alter the synthesis and metabolism of cholesterol in the liver.

Foods containing soy protein include soy milk, tofu, meat substitutes (such as vegetable burgers) and baked goods made with soy flour. Because soy protein occurs in or can be added to a wide variety of foods and beverages, it is possible to eat soy protein-containing products as many as 4 times a day (3 meals and a snack), according to the FDA.

Studies show 25 grams of soy protein per day have a cholesterol-lowering effect. Therefore, for a food to qualify for the health claim, each serving of the food must contain at least 6.25 grams of soy protein, or one-fourth of the 25-gram amount shown to have a cholesterol-lowering effect.

Soyfoods USA, Vol. 2, No. 11   December 16, 1997

SOY PROTEIN LOWERS RISK FOR CORONARY HEART DISEASE

Research about soy protein and heart disease was presented recently at the American Dietetic Association 80th Annual Meeting and Exhibition, held October 27-30, 1997, in Boston, Massachusetts. In his presentation, Dr. James W. Anderson, M.D., Professor of Medicine and Clinical Nutrition, University of Kentucky, concludes that:

"Soy protein and its isoflavones provide many health benefits. Careful studies indicate that regular intake of soy protein is associated with favorable changes in serum lipoprotein concentrations. Our meta-analysis noted that soy protein intake was accompanied by a significant 12.9% reduction in LDL-cholesterol levels, a significant 10% reduction in serum triglycerides and a 2.4% increase in serum HDL-cholesterol values."

Dr.Anderson's recommendations for general prevention of atherosclerotic cardiovascular disease are: "For persons in good general health, a suggestion is to have 7 servings of soy protein per week. This would provide an average of approximately 8 to 10 grams soy protein daily with 16-20 mg of soy isoflavones daily. This could be obtained from 8 oz. of a soy beverage daily or two soy muffins daily or two servings of tofu four times weekly or four soy burgers weekly or 1 tablespoon (14 g.) of isolated soy protein stirred into beverage daily.

A written version of Dr. Anderson's presentation, as well as his estimated value for isoflavone content of selected soyfoods can be found at the U. S. Soyfoods Directory Web site http://soyfoods.com/Anderson.html.

SOY-BASED ESTROGEN MAY ALLOW LOWER DOSES

In a December 8 article published by Reuters, it was reported that women who cannot tolerate side effects of hormone replacement therapy might be able to derive the same benefits with a half dose of a plant-based estrogen. Researchers at the University of California found post-menopausal woman given half the normal dose of Estratab showed improved bone density.

Unlike most estrogen supplements, derived from the urine of pregnant horses, the Estratab used in the study is made from soy and yams, according to the Reuters article. Currently Estratab is marketed only as a drug to relieve side effects of menopause such as hot flashes.

Solvay Pharmaceuticals, the Marietta, Georgia, company that makes Estratab, has asked the Food and Drug Administration to approve it in a broader indication to prevent osteoporosis, and submitted the trial data in support of its application.

HIGH SOY INTAKE LINKED TO LOW CHOLESTEROL LEVELS

Individuals who have a high soy intake have lower cholesterol levels than those who consume less soy, according to Japanese researchers in a report published recently in Tokyo. Dr. Hiroyuki Shimizu, of the Department of Public Health at Gifu University School of Medicine, and colleagues examined the relationship between intake of soy products and total serum cholesterol concentrations in 1,242 men and 3,596 women who participated in an annual health check-up program in Takayama City, Japan.

Among men, Dr. Shimizu's group observed a significant trend for decreasing total cholesterol concentrations with an increased intake of soy products after controlling for age, smoking status, and intake of total energy, total protein, and total fat. They noted a similar negative trend in women.

SOY COMPOUND ACTS LIKE ESTROGEN

In a recent Reuters article http://www.reutershealth.com it was reported that "the estrogen-like compounds found in soy—known as phytoestrogens—appear to be as effective as the estrogen found in hormone replacement therapies at slowing progression of atherosclerosis (clogging of the arteries), according to a study in monkeys." The finding was presented recently at the American Heart Association's 38th Annual Conference on Cardiovascular Disease Epidemiology and Prevention in Santa Fe, New Mexico.

The research was conducted by Mary Anthony and Dr. Thomas Clarkson of Bowman Gray School of Medicine in Winston-Salem http//www.bgsm.edu/.

LET'S GO SOYFOODS SHOPPING!

(Where to find soyfoods in your supermarket or health food store)

By Kim Galeaz, RD Nutrition Consultant to the Indiana Soybean Board kimgaleaz@aol.com

More and more of you want to know WHERE to find soyfoods in the supermarket or health food store. So we are listing the most common areas where you'll find your favorite soyfoods. Keep in mind it will differ from store to store, but these basic tips will help you fill your grocery cart with phytochemical-rich soyfoods!

Check all the areas suggested and then as a last resort: ask, ask, ask for help in locating these foods! Supermarket clerks and managers would rather be asked question after question than have you leave the store empty-handed because you can't find the item in the area you think it should be. And, don't forget, you can always order soyfoods online, too. You can find a listing at the U. S. Soyfoods Directory http://www.soyfoods.com/SoyfoodsOnline.html.

Soy Flour...Supermarket

1. Health foods section of large supermarkets.

2. Regular baking goods aisle next to all the other flours.

3. Self-standing display in the center of the aisle or display at the end of the regular aisles. This is common when one company wants to display all the items in their line of products.

...Health/natural food store

1. Flour area - both packaged and bulk food section

Soy Milk...Supermarket

1. Health foods section of many supermarkets—dry or refrigerated.

2. Refrigerated dairy milk section of supermarket, may be on shelf right nearby, even though the aseptic cartons don't need refrigerating until opened.
3. New brands and varieties of soymilk are packed in paper 1/2 gallons just like dairy milk and is perishable. This needs refrigeration before and after opening.

...Health/natural food store

1. Specialty milk area on shelves

2. Refrigerator case (although the aseptic cartons do not need refrigerating until open)

Soynut Butter...Supermarket
1. Health foods section

2. May be near the peanut butter

...Health/natural food store

1. Specialty spreads and nut butters area on shelf

Tofu - Water Packed...Supermarket

1. Produce area along with vegetables, fruits, and/or salads.

2. Refrigerated case in health foods section

3. Asian ethnic sections in large supermarkets with specific Japanese and Chinese areas.

...Health/natural food store

1. Refrigerated case

Tofu - Aseptic Packages...Supermarket

1. Health foods section on the shelf

2. Health foods section in the refrigerated case (although it doesn't need refrigeration until opened).

3. Produce department (although it doesn't need refrigeration until opened).

4. Asian ethnic sections in large supermarkets with specific Japanese and Chinese areas.

...Health/natural food store

1. Shelves with other main dish foods

2. Refrigerated case

Soy Cheeses...Supermarket

1. Health foods section refrigerated case

2. Along with all the other cheeses in grocery in refrigerated case

...Health/natural food store

1. Refrigerator case

Tempeh... Supermarket

1. Refrigerated case of health foods section

2. In extremely large supermarkets with vast ethnic areas you'll find tempeh in the Asian sections in the refrigerated cases.

...Health/natural food store

1. Refrigerated case

Meat Alternatives (soy burgers, soy crumbles, hot dogs, sausages, etc.)....Supermarket

1. Freezer case aisles along with all the other frozen burgers, sausages, ground meat items, and even breakfast foods. In some stores, specific brands of these items are all displayed together. So you may need to check ALL of the freezer cases to find ALL of the different brands that store carries.

2. Health foods section freezer case

...Health/natural food store

1. Freezer case

Textured Soy Protein (dry products)...Supermarket

1. Health foods section sold plain in bags or boxes. Or mixed with other ingredients and sold in boxes as "quick & easy" meals, like "chili mix" or Sloppy Joe mix.

2. May be mixed in the baking products aisle along with flours and other ingredients.

...Health/natural food store

1. Bulk area

2. Shelves with other dry products

Roasted Soynuts... Supermarket

1. Health foods section

2. Snacks/chips/nuts area of supermarket

...Health/natural food store

1. Bulk foods area

2. Snack foods area

Whole Soybeans. . .Supermarket

1. Health foods section in cans or bags on shelf

2. Bulk foods section

3. On the shelf next to all the other canned beans, like navy and kidney beans.

...Health/natural food store

1. Bulk foods section

2. Canned foods aisle on shelf

Green Soybeans...Supermarket

1. Freezer case near all other frozen bagged vegetables. Labeled as "edamame" or simply "green soybeans."
2. Right now in many US markets, you can purchase a specific brand of mixed vegetables that contains green soybeans as one of the ingredients. It's called "Baby Broccoli Blend" by Freshlike and it features "Sweet Beans", the Freshlike trademark name for green soybeans. This vegetable blend contains broccoli, water chestnuts and carrots in as well as the green sweet soybeans. It tastes terrific!!

3. In extremely large supermarkets with vast ethnic areas, you'll find these in the Japanese/ Chinese/Asian sections in the frozen food cases.

...Health/natural food store

1. Freezer case with other vegetables and frozen foods

Soy Frozen Desserts. . .Supermarket

1. Health foods freezer case

2. Frozen foods aisle with other dessert/ice cream products

...Health/natural food store

1. Freezer case

SOYFOODS ARE HIGH IN IRON

Iron deficiency is the most common nutritional problem in the world. In the United States, it is most often seen in toddlers, teens, and in young and pregnant women.

Low iron intake results in anemia. People with this condition often suffer from fatigue, headaches, and increased risk of infection. Many foods are rich in iron, but many whole plant foods are especially good sources. Vegetarians and others who eat plant-based diets actually have the highest iron intakes. In fact, the more the diet is based on plant foods, the higher the intake of iron.

However, the amount of iron in the diet is only part of the story. The amount of iron that is actually absorbed into the bloodstream is also very important.

Soyfoods USA Vol. 1 No. 12   January 16, 1997

GETTING SOY INTO SCHOOL LUNCH PROGRAM

Soy-enhanced meat and poultry products hit a home run with the toughest food critics around—more than 11,000 school lunch customers. In a recent nationwide pilot program designed to measure student acceptability of soy-enhanced meat and poultry products, students in six economically and geographically diverse school districts rated 17 different soy-enhanced foods ranging from chicken patties to chili to submarine sandwiches.

"While many school foodservice directors understand soy is a low-fat protein source, they don't serve soy products because they mistakenly think kids won't eat them," said Anita Say-Holquist, school foodservice director of the Oakland Unified School district in Oakland, California. "I think people's connotation of soy is incorrect. As a participant of the national pilot program, we found students like soy enhanced foods." The Oakland district serves 30,000 lunches and 8,000 breakfasts per day.

More than half of the students surveyed in taste tests gave the soy entrees a score of five on a five-point scale. Overall, 67 percent of students rated the entrees as above average.

Some soy enhanced foods were especially popular with the kids. "Once students find something they like, they will ask for it. In junior high, the cold cuts went over very well," explains Holquist. "In fact, the students asked for the products again after the test."

Plate waste survey of nearly 5,000 students show students do more than ask for soy-enhanced foods—they eat them. According to the plate waste surveys conducted in the six pilot districts, 65 percent of students ate all of the soy-enhanced entree on their plate. Another 22 percent ate at least half.

The pilot tests focused on soy-enhanced meat products, which contain up to 30 percent soy protein. As a result of the program, some of the participating schools say they plan to add soy-enhanced foods to their menus.

In the Corpus Christi, Texas, Independent School District, foodservice director Jodi Houston said her district plans to implement five soy-enhanced menu items, including spaghetti with meat sauce, lasagna and tacos, this year. The district serves 35,000 lunches per day.

"The addition of soy to the recipes we plan to add to our menu decreases the fat content and increases the dietary fiber of each dish. This helps my district meet the recommended dietary guidelines for Americans," said Houston.

Building upon the success of the pilot program, the United Soybean Board (USB) is sponsoring seminars throughout the nation to demonstrate how incorporating more soy protein in school meals will allow directors to cut the fat—but not the taste—from school lunches in a cost-effective way.

The seminars, entitled "Reinventing the Meal with Soy!" will also give directors an opportunity to see how soy protein has improved in quality and consistency since its introduction to school foodservice in the 70's.

Learning how to add soy protein to menu items is as simple as attending a seminar. Nutritionists will demonstrate easy steps for preparing lower-fat versions of existing recipes, as well as provide suggestions for incorporating soy-enhanced foods in meal plans. Participants will receive a free information kit, which includes student-tested recipes and menu plans, cost comparisons, nutritional analysis, product and vendor information, and promotional materials. Seminar attendees will receive two hours of continuing education credit from the American School Food Service Association.

For more information, or to inquire about the conferences, please contact Nabeeha M. Kazi or Rebecca Cisek kazin@fleishman.com, Fleisbman-Hillard, 816-474-9407.

Soyfoods Nutrition Information

Although soyfoods are widely recognized for their nutritional qualities, interest in soyfoods has risen recently because scientists have discovered that a soy component called isoflavones appears to reduce the risk of cancer. More research needs to be done to determine exactly how isoflavones work, but it appears that as little as one serving of soyfoods a day may be enough to obtain the benefits of this anticancer phytochemical.

The calcium content of fortified soymilks, which may be found in retail stores, can be found in our Soymilk Calcium Chart.

It is important, though, to understand the entire nutritional value of specific soyfoods so that dietetic decisions can be made. For instance, soy protein has been found to be effective in reducing cholesterol, in treating kidney disease, and may cause calcium to be better utilized, helping to ward off osteoporosis. Some soyfoods, such as miso, contain high amounts of sodium, and should be avoided by people who need to minimize their sodium intake. A single serving of tempeh contains twice as much fiber as the average American eats in a day.

Soymilk Calcium Chart

Soymilk that has been fortified with calcium is your best choice for getting significant amounts of calcium. Since all soymilk is not fortified, you should read the nutrition information on labels carefully. Use the following chart to help you get a jump start on the right soymilk for you. Remember, it is still wise to read the food label since food companies may reformulate their products.

The daily value for calicum is 1 gram for adults and children age 4 or older. This is equal to 1,000 milligrams. If the Nutrition Facts on a soymilk container states, "Calcium 20 percent," then you know the amount of calicum for one serving of soymilk is 200 milligrams, or 20 percent of the recommended daily value for adults and older children.

Brand & Flavor	Milligrams of calcium per 1 cup	Calories per 1 cup	Grams of protein 1 cup	Grams of fat 1 cup
EdenSoy Extra Original	200	130	10	4
EdenSoy Extra Vanilla	200	150	6	3
Fat-Free Soy Moo	400	110	6	0
Westsoy Plus Plain	300	130	6	4
Westsoy Plus Vanilla	300	150	6	4
Westsoy Plus Cocoa	300	190	6	4
Westsoy Lowfat Plain	200	90	4	2
Westsoy Lowfat Vanilla	200	120	4	2
Westsoy Non Fat Plain	200	80	3	0
Westsoy Non Fat Vanilla	200	80	3	0
Silk (always found in a refrigerated case)	300	80	4	2.5
Silk Chocolate	300	100	4	2.5
Pacific Lite Plain	300	100	4	2.5
Pacific Lite Vanilla	300	110	4	2.5
Pacific Lite Cocoa	350	160	4	2
Pacific Ultra-Plus Plain	300	160	6	5
Pacific Ultra-Plus Vanilla	300	170	6	5
Solair Original (dry instant made from soybeans)	300	110	5	3

Brand & Flavor	Milligrams of calcium per 1 cup	Calories per 1 cup	Grams of protein 1 cup	Grams of fat 1 cup
Solair Chocolate	200	114	5	3
Solair Vanilla Bean	200	98	3	2
Better Than Milk? Plain Light (dry instant made from tofu)	500	80	2	5
Better Than Milk? Vanilla	500	90	2	5
Better Than Milk? Plain	80	100	2	2.5
Better Than Milk? Carob	350	114	2	2
Better Than Milk? Chocolate	350	98	1	2

SOY: THE NEXT THERAPY FOR OSTEOPOROSIS?

When it comes to preventing or maybe even treating osteoporosis, natural sources of calcium--such as dairy foods, beans and dark green vegetables--may have some new natural allies: soyfoods.

For years, physicians and nutritionists have emphasized the consumption of calcium-rich foods as a way to prevent osteoporosis, the loss of bone mass and strength. It is estimated that as many as 24 million Ameicans, both men and women, have some degree of osteoporosis. Once osteoporosis has occurred, especially after menopause, therapies have included drugs which inhibit or slow bone loss.

An Illinois Soybean Checkoff Board (ISCB)-funded a study at the University of Illinois-Chicago (UIC). This study has shown that soy protein may lead to a "natural" therapy for osteoporosis sufferers. The research project examined whether soy protein isolate, a highly concentrated form of soy protein often used in processed foods like breads, meat products and drinks, would prevent or even slow bone loss.

The researchers found that soy protein, or its yet-to-be-determined components, was important in protecting bone mass. Rats fed soy protein in the study had a higher rate of turnover-bone formation exceeding bone resorption—an important finding not only to post-menopausal women but to an aging population. As people age, bone turnover slows, leading to a greater incidence of fractures

Bahram Arjmandi Ph.D., R.D., principal investigator in the study, said that soy protein has affected even more than bone density. "We found that while bone density increased with the consumption of soy isolate, more importantly, bone quality was improved. This is very important to the growing population of Americans confronting the onset of osteoporosis."

Researchers are seeking additional government funding to continue this study with a two-year clinical trial of post-menopausal women. The human study will seek to confirm the results of the laboratory trials and also will try to determine the specific soy component that improves bone density and enhances bone quality.

NEW RESEARCH ON PHYTOESTROGENS AND BREAST CANCER

Consuming a diet rich in naturally-occurring plant chemicals called phytoestrogens may decrease the risk of breast cancer, according to a Reuters report this month about a new study done in Australia. According to the article, "women with high levels of two phytoestrogen byproducts--equol and enterolactone--in their urine had a lower risk of breast cancer compared with other women." This information is significant for people who consume soyfoods, since they are an important source of phytoestrogens.

A copy of the article can be found on the World Wide Web at: http://www.yahoo.com/headlines/971006/health/stories/diet_l.html

SOYFOODS REDUCE THE RISK OF OSTEOPOROSIS

Eating soyfoods may be one easy way to help build strong bones and to lower risk of osteoporosis. Osteoporosis involves thinning and weakening of bones and is a very serious and common problem throughout the world.

Osteoporosis is most often seen in older people since bones become thinner, weaker, and brittle with aging. The United States has one of the world's highest rates of osteoporosis. Between 15 and 20 million Americans suffer from this disease. Women are more likely than men to have poor bone health. One out of every five American women over the age of 65 has factured one or more bones.

The good news is lifestyle changes can greatly aid bone health. For example, exercise is very important for developing strong bones and for keeping bones from getting thin. Physical activity can slow the loss of bone matter that occurs with aging. In fact, exercise not only slows bone loss in the elderly, it actually leads to an increase in bone density.

A healthy diet is also important for strong bones. Some dietary factors, like caffeine, sodium, and protein may speed bone loss. Nutrients, like calcium and vitamin D, help promote bone health. Adding soybeans and soyfoods to the diet may also help reduce risk of osteoporosis. Soyfoods may work in three ways to protect the health of bones:

■ Many soyfoods are rich in calcium.

■ Soy protein helps conserve calcium in the body.

■ Compounds in soybeans may protect the strength of bones.

Soyfoods Provide Calcium

The best protection against osteoporosis in later life is having strong, dense bones early in life. Adequate calcium intake is crucial for this.

Although most people think of milk first as a source of calcium, many foods are rich in this nutrient. Legumes, such as soybeans, are naturally good sources of calcium. One cup of cooked soybeans contains about 12 percent of the adult calcium recommended daily allowance. Some brands of tofu are especially rich in calcium because they are made with a calcium salt. The calcium in soyfoods is very well absorbed by the body.

Soy Protein Helps Conserve Calcium

The bones are very dynamic as they constantly break down and rebuild. Some calcium is lost from the body every day and a new supply of calcium must come from the diet. As important as adequate calcium intake is, it is equally, or perhaps more, important to reduce the amount of calcium being lost from the body. A high intake of dietary protein can increase the loss of calcium and this may raise risk of osteoporosis. But all protein isn't equal in this regard. Studies show that soy protein does not have the same calcium-wasting effect. When people eat soyfoods in place of animal proteins, they excrete far less calcium in their urine.

Compounds in Soybeans Protect Bone Health

Soybeans are a unique source of a group of compounds called isoflavones. Soybeans are the only food that contain these compounds in significant amounts. One type of isoflavone called daidzein is very similar to a drug widely used in Asia and Europe to treat osteoporosis. This drug prevents bone from breaking down. When the drug is metabolized in the body, it produces daidzein—the same compound found in soybeans. This suggests that eating soyfoods—natural sources of daidzein—

could help reduce the risk of osteoporosis. But another isoflavone in soyfoods, genistein, may help. In one recent animal study, genistein was also shown to inhibit breakdown of bone.

A Bone-Healthy Lifestyle

Many factors affect bone health. A lifestyle that promotes healthy bones includes the following:

√ **Exercise.** Weight-bearing exercise, such as walking and running, is one of the most important factors affecting bone health.

√ **Adequate intake of calcium.** Choose calcium-rich foods often. They include dark green leafy vegetables, broccoli, Chinese cabbage, many legumes (especially black beans, chickpeas, and baked beans), almonds, figs, fortified orange juice, dairy products and soyfoods such as tofu made with calcium salts, fortified soy milk, tempeh, textured vegetable protein, and cooked soybeans.

√ **Moderate protein intake.** Avoid excessive animal protein by eating more grains, beans, fruits, and vegetables.

√ **Limited sodium intake.** Most sodium comes from processed foods.

√ **Add soyfoods to diet.** Because many soyfoods provide calcium, are rich in the type of protein that does not induce calcium loss and are a source of isoflavones, they provide a unique way to improve bone health.

THE SOYFOODS FAMILY

The extended family of the soybean ranges from ancient and traditional Asian fare, such as tofu and tempeh, to products that mimic all-American favorites like soy-based hot dogs and meatless burgers. Here are a few of the major soyfoods that can be found in the U.S. Soyfoods Directory http://soyfoods.com/

Soybeans: These legumes grow in fuzzy pods and are nearly always available as a dried product. The dried beans must be soaked for six to eight hours and then cooked until tender, about two hours (or 15 minutes in a pressure cooker). They have a somewhat nutty flavor that is especially delicious in barbecue-type sauces or tomato-flavored sauces. Always add tomatoes near the end of the cooking cycle since they toughen soybeans and make them difficult to cook. The immature, green beans are sometimes available frozen or fresh. Cook them for 15 to 20 minutes and serve as a vegetable.

Roasted soynuts: These are a crunchy snack food made by roasting soaked soybeans until browned.

Textured soy protein: Usually sold as textured vegetable protein or TVP, these dried granules of compressed soy flour must be rehydrated with boiling water (7/8 cup boiling water poured over 1 cup TVP) before using. It has a texture like ground beef and is delicious in tomato-based products like chili, sloppy joes, and spaghetti sauce.

Soy flour: Available as a full-fat or defatted product, this flour can be paired with wheat flour or other flours in a variety of baked goods.

Soy milk: Made from the liquid expressed from soaked soybeans, it is usually sweetened and sometimes flavored with chocolate, carob or vanilla, and is a good replacement for cow's milk in a wide variety of dishes. Both regular and reduced-fat versions are available.

Tofu: This delicate curd is made by adding a mineral salt to soy milk and then pressing the curds together into a solid block. The flavor is quite bland, but tofu takes on the flavor of whatever it is cooked with, and is useful in any type of dish from a spicy entree to the richest, sweetest dessert. Both firm and soft tofu are available, as well as a more custard-like product called silken tofu.

Tempeh: The whole soybean is fermented to produce a soft block of beans that has a rich, smoky flavor. Tempeh can be barbecued or used as a meat replacement in stews and casseroles.

Miso: This is a salty paste made from soybeans and grains. It is used to flavor broths and often is used in place of soy sauce.

Meat and Dairy Analogues: A wide variety of foods made from tofu and other soy products resemble foods like cheese,yogurt, burgers, hot dogs, and luncheon and breakfast meats. They can be used in the same ways as the foods they mimic.

Soyfoods USA Vol 1 No 11   December 16, 1996

FIRST ANNUAL SOYFOODS SYMPOSIUM

The First Annual Soy Symposium held November 19 & 20, 1996 at Paducah, Kentucky was well attended by more people than originally expected from around the country. This Symposium was the first of a yearly program sponsored by the Kentucky Soybean Association for dietitians, school food service professionals, and food manufacturers. Overall, the speakers and sessions were well-received, and, judging by comments overheard at the symposium, much new information was gleaned by attendants.

Kim Galeaz, RD, nutrition consultant to the Indiana Soybean Development Council, interviewed a renal dietitian, a cardiology diet technician, and an elementary school cafeteria manager for their observations. They were pleasantly surprised by how much they learned about soyfoods. Here's Kim's report...

"The conference was exciting because I learned that soy protein does not raise the glomerular filtration rate for pre-end stage renal patients, like regular high biological value proteins, like eggs and chicken," said Carol Durbin, RD, a renal dietitian at Indiana Nephrology & Internal Medicine in Indianapolis. Durbin says she intends to begin recommending soyfoods to her renal patients because the soy protein isn't as taxing on the kidneys. For renal patients this may mean a longer period of time without having to go on kidney dialysis. Durbin was also delighted to learn soy protein is a complete protein, making it a great protein source for all renal patients.

This was Durbin's first soy conference, and she was glad to hear a presentation by Anne Patterson, RD. Patterson described many different kinds of soyfoods, how to buy them, store them and cook them—a very practical presentation for many people in the audience. "I was impressed with everything Patterson shared about cooking and using all the different soyfoods," said Durbin. She now feels more comfortable with adding a few soyfoods to her diet, as well as the diets of her patients. And Durbin admits it's easier than she thought to try to add one or two soyfoods a day!

Susan Becker, DTR, a diet technician and health promotions manager at Nasser, Smith & Pinkerton Cardiology in Indianapolis, concurs with Durbin's observations. After listening to Dr. James Anderson from the University of Kentucky talk about the numerous studies indicating that soy protein in the diet lowers cholesterol levels, Becker says she feels more confident recommending soyfoods to her cardiac patients.

In her search for new soyfoods she could recommend to her clients, Becker was impressed with Harvest Burger for Recipes at the "Taste of Soy" trade show during the soy symposium and really liked the flavor. "I've even asked my local supermarket to stock the item so I can buy it regularly," Becker said. Harvest Burger for Recipes is sold under the Green Giant label and is basically soy protein in a "crumbles" form, similar to ground beef. It should be available at most supermarkets nationwide. Becker believes this product would be easy for many heart patients to use because it can be used in soups, chili, casseroles and taco mixes.

Barbara Diefenbach, Cafeteria Manager at Lillian Emory Elementary School in New Albany, Indiana, heard about soyfoods and their benefits for the very first time at this Kentucky soy symposium. "I had no idea soyfoods were so good for you!" said Diefenbach. All the speakers and presentations at this symposium were her first exposure to the relationship of soyfoods to heart disease, diabetes, kidney disease, and even osteoporosis. "I'd really like to use more foods in our cafeteria that have some soy in them," Diefenbach explained. She believes it would be good to encourage children to eat more soyfoods when they are younger, and she intends to search for more menu items that contain soy protein.

Diefenbach especially liked hearing how a food service manager in Kentucky added numerous soyfoods to her menu.

Soyfoods USA Vol. 3 No. 4   May 16, 1998

SOYBEAN-DERIVED DRUG TO BE TESTED ON BREAST CANCER PATENTS

A soybean-derived molecule that acts like a smart bomb by seeking out cancer cells and interfering with their ability to survive and multiply is set to be tested on late-stage breast cancer patients, according to an article in the Twin Cities Star-Tribune. Researcher Dr. Fatih Uckun, said the molecule has caused human breast tumors transplanted into mice to shrivel up and die. The molecule blocks the action of an enzyme that tumor cells need to survive and multiply, Uckun said. His findings appear in the April issue of the journal Clinical Cancer Research. http:/webserv.startribune.corn/May-98

NEW STUDY SHOWS GENISTEIN MAY INHIBIT CANCER

A new university study on the anti-cancer effects of soy has found that one of soy's components, genistein, may inhibit the growth of cancer cells. The new study is from the University of Southern California's School of Medicine and is titled Mechanism for the Suppression of the Mammalian Stress Response by Genistein, an Anti-cancer Phytoestrogen from Soy." It found that genistein suppresses the production of harmful stress proteins in cells; these stress proteins, which include heat shock proteins (HSPs) and glucose-regulated proteins (GRPs), normally help cancer cells survive destruction by the immune system.

An article about the study can be found at http://biz.yahoo.com/ prnews/980424/dc_soy_stu_l.html.

COMPARING THE COST OF SOYFOODS

By Kim Galeaz, R
Nutrition Consultant to the Indiana Soybean Board/
Kimgaleaz@aol.com

Often I'm asked "Why do soyfoods cost so much more than regular foods?" When I pose the question to soyfoods manufacturers, I am usually given one of several answers:

1. Although soyfoods are increasingly popular because of recent research findings and new processing techniques that have greatly increased their taste appeal to American consumers, most soyfoods simply are not produced in sufficient quantity to achieve the same economies of scale associated with more traditional foods.

2. Most specialty foods will always be a little more costly, again because they are produced in lower quantities, and soyfoods are still considered specialty foods in many areas.

3. Where you purchase the item makes a price difference. Where the sales volume is a little higher, such as in natural or health food stores, soyfoods may be sold at a more competitive, lower price than in a supermarket.

My answer always includes these reasons, but I also tell people that not all soyfoods are expensive, and some soyfoods are even less expensive than their more traditional counterparts. To find out just how much soyfoods cost, I recently surveyed several stores and compared prices. The results may surprise you. For instance, I found that soynuts may cost anywhere from $0.96 to $2.59 per pound, but peanuts can cost $3.39 to $3.79 per pound. Cashews can cost a whopping $7.85 per pound! There is no doubt that other soyfoods, such as soymilk, may cost a little more, but I believe the added benefits are well worth the cost.

I'M A SOY NUT!

By Bonnie Terrill Ross, MS, RD
Indianapolis, Indiana

Ironic Memories

I was a keynote speaker for a community forum on cancer many years ago. During a break after my presentation, a soyfoods fanatic overtook me. He dominated my space with gushy health claims on soyfoods. I confess, I pegged him as a well-meaning but misguided zealot. Since this person was not a health professional, I foolishly concluded the subject of soyfoods and health benefits were not worth any serious consideration.

Ah, isn't life ironic? Almost a decade later, I have become wildly excited about the health benefits from soyfoods. The staff in my department fondly call me the "soy queen," and my family is becoming predictable at supper time. They will raise one eyebrow and inquire "soy again?"

Looking Back and Learning Forward

My story has taught me not to be so arrogant about nutrition issues I am unfamiliar with. Our traditional training as dietitians is shallow in many areas. It's through our perseverance, our professional experiences, digging into the scientific literature, and truly learning about (not just politely acknowledging) our herbal heritage and international cultural nutritional differences with health and disease that we begin to appreciate the vast, complicated science of nutrition, health, and disease.

I think I tend to be a bit thick-headed, but I compensate with my insatiable curiosity and lots of determination. I have tracked cutting edge trends in nutrition sciences, such as immunonutrition, chemoprevention, and phytochemicals. I have made presentations at countless professional workshops and seminars.

In 1994, I attended a fascinating workshop at the University of Michigan on Nutrition and Cancer Prevention. After that, my interest in phytochemicals exploded. A few months later I read "The Simple Soybean," by Mark Messina, PhD and Virginia Messina, RD. The book and the workshop have been a real turning point in my approach to nutrition. They somehow have solidified the nutrition logic I have sought, backed with the solid scientific data that I demand.

Compelling Health Benefits

The health benefits from soyfoods are remarkable! So much so that it could be easy to dismiss them as too good (or too easy) to be true! As an oncology dietitian, my interest naturally started with soy protein's link with cancer. I have learned that cultures that include soyfoods as a regular part of their diet have fewer cancers, especially breast and prostate cancer. Numerous epidemiological studies have found a lower risk for colon, rectal, lung, and stomach cancer with soyfood consumption. And it appears that as little as one serving of soyfood a day offers protection from cancers.

Soyfoods offer these benefits because they contain various groups of chemicals that are protective against cancer. More than 100 in vitro studies have found that the isoflavone, genistein, in soy protein inhibits the growth of a wide range of cancer cells.

Soy protein benefits are well established and should be included in cardiac education programs. Soy protein has been shown to directly lower blood cholesterol, inhibit LDL-cholesterol oxidation (in vitro studies show it may inhibit platelet aggregation). As with most issues on nutrition and chronic diseases, the diet and lifestyle needs to be approached globally. Advocating a plant based diet rich in grains, legumes, vegetables, and fruit and low in fat, sodium, and processed foods, along with healthy behaviors such as exercise and abstinence from tobacco and alcohol excess is paramount with health education.

Hormone Changes and Hot Flashes

The isoflavones in soyfoods may help to reduce some of the problems associated with menopause. About 75 percent of

American women experience night sweats and/or hot flashes during the perimenopausal years. Japanese women, whose diets contain many soyfoods, rarely experience hot flashes or sleep disturbances in their perimenopausal years. The Japanese language does not even have a word to describe hot flashes.

Isoflavones have a chemical structure very similar to estrogen and are found in meaningful amounts only in soyfoods. The weak estrogen activity of soy protein is felt to relieve hot flash symptoms that occur with menopause because of the body's declining production of estrogen. Various studies are underway to further assess this relationship.

Most breast cancers are considered to be estrogen dependent, as well. This is the theory behind the dramatically lower incidence of breast cancer in women who regularly consume soyfoods. The isoflavones in soyfoods are protective (anti-estrogenic) against breast cancer because they "block" the potent endogenous estrogen. Since the isoflavones also are very weak estrogens, they provide enough activity (estrogenic) to offset menopause symptoms and protect the cardiovascular system, help prevent osteoporosis, and lessen menopausal symptoms.

Soyfoods with Cancer Patients on Hormones

In my oncology practice, many of the breast cancer patients are on Tamoxifen which is an estrogen antagonist. The Tamoxifen is prescribed as a means to control breast cancer. Most women are scheduled to stay on this five years. Also, women with breast cancer are rarely allowed to ever take HRT (hormone replacement therapy). Hot flashes are very common with Tamoxifen and some women will not comply with this important drug because of miserable hot flashes.

We have initiated a protocol in our practice to teach breast cancer patients on Tamoxifen who are suffering from hot flashes to incorporate soyfoods in their daily diet. We then monitor their soyfoods compliance and hot flashes for six months. Most women have noted some improvement ranging from slight to dramatic. As we enroll more women and assess results, we will get a stronger clinical feel.

We also started a similar protocol for men with prostate cancer who have received hormonal blockade as a part of their disease control. These men often experience intense hot flashes and night sweats. Our results thus far have been dramatically impressive! Until our experiences broaden, and there are clinical trials, final conclusions cannot be drawn.

My protocol patients feel empowered by their experience with soyfoods. They are eager to share tips and experiences. I receive several calls from our soy protocol patients whenever soyfoods are in the news. The recent article on isoflavones and hot flashes in the August 1996 Prevention magazine prompted many women to call me to make sure that I got a copy.

Teaching patients how to incorporate isoflavone rich soyfoods in their daily diet initially was a challenge because many people are unfamiliar with this food. But after 15 months of teaching patients about soyfoods, I have gained my rightful title of "Soy Queen!"

I have developed a package of information that includes numerous recipes and tips about how to incorporate soyfoods into your diet. The compliance has been wonderful. Every patient we have entered into this protocol has considered the incorporation of soyfoods to be easy! The soy milk and soy nuts are particularly well liked, especially for those who do not enjoy working with recipes. The staff and physicians I work with are often sampling soyfood recipes that I have made, and I have converted many of them! As patients have completed our protocol schedule, every one thus far intends to continue to regularly consume soyfoods on their own!

My experience with soyfoods tells me that anyone with an interest can learn about how easy it is to add soyfoods to everyday diets.

Index